Confessions of an Illuminati Princess

Christy Zagami

Cursum Perfiscio

Contents

This book is dedicated to Nick and Tony

Forward

A few years ago, it would have seemed impossible, but I am happy about this incredible development that has proven Christy to be a talented writer and the opportunity she has given me, a true honor, to write the foreword for her first book.

My father, the late Elio Zagami, once told me after meeting Christy for the first time, that she was a magical person, and I must admit he was totally right in stating this to me back when I hardly knew her. Having her next to me for nearly a decade has changed my life into the most wonderful adventure that completely erases the many difficulties we encountered along the way because of my enemies. I am finally happy, especially after I had in the years prior to meeting Christy, what can be considered the worst experience a man can ever have, the one of being betrayed and sold to a corrupt system by the people you loved, and who were supposed to love you.

Being persecuted and arrested in Norway for exposing the inner secrets of the dark cabal that rules the world with hypocrisy and lies was a dramatic experience for me. Later on, I was institutionalized, something they used in the past to discredit me, and I am probably one of the few people in the world that had to suffer an accusation for espionage in one country (Norway), and at the same time, treated as a mental case in another (Italy). The two should not be legally compatible and I hope to have enough money one day to sue both the Italian and Norwegian judicial systems for their unjust persecution.

The left-wing criminals of the Obama/Clinton era wanted me dead for exposing their secret ties to Satanism with their Muslim allies. In the end, with Christy's help and her constant support, I managed not only to survive, but also to write and publish many books all over the world with great success. Having said this, I had little hope for the future in 2008, I even thought about suicide many times, when I finally asked the universe, after my latest arrest for espionage in Norway, to send an angel to save me, and when she finally arrived, she was the sweetest and most beautiful angel a man could ever ask for.

Ad Maiora.
Leo Lyon Zagami

Introduction

I have been in a relationship for almost 10 years with a man who has put his life on the line by exposing the evil of the New World Order. It's not only his life, but mine too, as many times the attacks are directed at me because the evil ones know that is the best way to get to Leo. In the beginning, I was scared, and I spent a lot of time worried that the door would be smashed down and Leo taken away after talking publicly on the radio and television. In the following pages, you will read, that things like this did indeed happen, and I had every reason to be afraid, but living my life in fear took a toll on me emotionally, spiritually, and even physically.

I couldn't go on like this, the stress was killing me. I decided that if I was going to continue to put myself in dangers way, I had to come to some kind of inner peace. I let go of my fears with the knowledge that what we are doing is important and that God will always protect us, therefore there is no reason to be afraid. We must all go forward to awaken as many people as we can, we are living a momentous time in history, *can you feel it?* We are all soldiers that must stand together and fight against the global evil that is trying to take us over. I believe we will win. Evil will not prevail! Welcome to the Confessions of an Illuminati Princess, and buckle up, because it's going to be a wild ride!

SOME SAY THERE IS NO DIFFERENCE BETWEEN LIGHT AND DARK - THAT THEY HAVE EQUAL POWER OVER THE SENSES. THE TRUTH IS THAT DARKNESS MUDDIES THE SENSES, MAKING IT DIFFICULT TO EVALUATE YOUR SURROUNDINGS, WHILE LIGHT ENHANCES YOUR SENSES GIVING YOU A PRISTINE VIEW. THIS CAN BE SAID OF YOUR SOUL. BY FOLLOWING THE LIGHTED PATH, YOU WILL ALWAYS HAVE A CLEAR VIEW OF WHO YOU ARE AND WHAT NEEDS TO BE DONE.

Ash Sweeney

Chapter 1

Welcome to my life

C rouched down in the corner of my closet I could hear the barrage of explosions echoing from the center of town. It was New Year's Eve and the world was celebrating. For some, the New Year represents a new beginning and perhaps a chance to start over, but this New Year's Eve I had never felt so lost and alone. In my secret place of isolation, I hugged the expensive bottle of Scotch I bought just for the occasion, as I cried bitterly to myself, I was happy to see the end of 2008.

It was a horrible year that I hadn't fully recovered from. As a matter of fact, the year before was pretty awful as well. I was living with an alcoholic and I was slowly becoming one myself. I still felt I had the problem under control and could stop drinking whenever I wanted, but it seemed I spent more and more afternoons drinking lately. It was my great escape. After a glass of whiskey, everything seemed fine. There were no more problems.

From the outside, I had the perfect life. My (first) husband was an air traffic controller, a stressful job that he held throughout our 18-year marriage. He began his air traffic control career as a U.S. Marine, where he set up mobile air traffic control bases in remote, usually dangerous places. I was left to care for two small children, 9 months out of the year, on my own. When he left the military in 2001 to begin a job with the FAA, I thought he would be around more, but it was just the opposite.

Air traffic control is one of the highest paid professions, but it also has the highest alcohol and suicide rate and most air traffic controllers are divorced at least once. You could say that the odds were stacked against me. I had abandonment and trust issues from childhood, but despite that, I always wanted to be a mother and have a family of my own. I treasured every moment I had with my children, from the time they were born, and I tried to show them the love that I felt I never received as a child. I wasn't perfect and I made a lot of mistakes. I was married at age 20, and I had two sons by the age of 23. While my sister and her friends were out clubbing and partying, I was at home changing diapers.

Me with my sister in Estes Park in 2008.

We had a few happy years in the beginning, but when my husband volunteered for a more dangerous career field, everything seemed to change. For his first deployment, he was gone for 6 months. I was young, but I tried to do the best I could. I didn't want my children to grow up like I did, the product of divorce.

That was until that fateful New Year's Eve, sitting at the bottom of my closet with an empty bottle of Scotch and no hope for the future. I knew I couldn't go on like this, something really bad would happen if I did. I had already begun to black out during some of my drinking sessions. I didn't want to hit rock bottom. I wanted to change my life for the better, I just didn't know how. I felt trapped in a life that I didn't want to live anymore.

My house in Estes Park.

We had more money than we ever had, but it was spent faster than my husband could make it. Money was spent on clothes, shoes, and material items in an attempt to fill the empty void inside of me. Most of the clothes I bought I didn't even wear, and they would remain hanging in my closet with the tags still on, months after purchasing them. From the corner of my closet where I had taken refuge, I stared up at all the beautiful items I had accumulated, and thought, *I would give it all up just to be happy.* It's true that money doesn't buy happiness, and I found that out the hard way. I squeezed my eyes shut and sent a prayer out to heaven to help me. *"Dear God, Please save me from this life, please send me an angel."* Little did I know that across the Atlantic, there was a man spending his New Year's Eve in a similar way, praying for an angel to save him...

∞ ∞ ∞

New Year's Day began like any other, except my hangover that morning was more intense, so I made the usual promise to myself that I wouldn't drink anymore. As I made breakfast for everyone, I began to count my blessings. I had a nice house and two beautiful kids. My marriage wasn't great, but it wasn't horrible either. I was relatively healthy, when so many suffered, so I decided I should just appreciate what I have, and that would be my New Year's resolution. I opened my laptop and decided to check my email. To my surprise, there was a message from a man, and he was Italian! I went over to my myspace account, something I had opened out of sheer boredom, and viewed the very polite, yet elaborate message. He was a lot more exciting and had a lot more to say than the usual messages that I received, so I quickly added him. There was a picture on his profile, and something inside me stirred when I saw it.

The first picture that I saw of Leo.

He mentioned a lot in his email that I didn't understand. It all seemed out of a Dan Brown movie, but I liked *The Da Vinci Code*, I had read it three times! He explained that he had found me through the profile of an Italian actress from my modeling days. He opened up a lot in that initial message, telling a virtual stranger how sad he was and how he prayed to God to send him an angel. I flashed back to the previous night, when I sent the same prayer out to the universe. I have always been a hopeless romantic and I believe in fate.

Leo in front of Castel Sant'Angelo photographer Gerald Bruneau.

Chapter 2

New York, New York, big city of dreams

My family on my mother's side was from Naples, Italy and had immigrated to America in the early 1900s. I spent the first 5 years of my life in Brooklyn, New York, and after my parent's divorce, I was sent back there to live with my grandmother from the age of 13 until 17. My years as a teenager in New York were wild, to say the least.

My father and brother lived with us for the first year, but my dad suffered a lot of mental problems, including severe PTSD, that surfaced after the divorce from my mother. I missed the way my family used to be, and I missed my mother and my sister, who were living in Colorado with my mother's new husband.

The first year in Brooklyn with my dad and my brother there were okay, but my world changed when my father announced one evening that he would be moving to Florida, and he would be taking my brother with him. I asked him if I could go too, but he refused, saying it would be rough living for a while, and it was no place for a girl.

He looked genuinely sad to say goodbye, but I still felt abandoned. I was 14 years old, trying desperately to accept all of the changes in my life that I had no control over. It was September 1985, and I had to face my first year of high school on my own. Many nights I cried myself to sleep, hugging my father's pillow. I felt so alone and sad, but I always enjoyed school and tried to focus on my classes.

Walking home one autumn day, a couple of weeks into the school year, I passed a row of houses, when a boy who sat behind me in three of my classes, a boy I happened to have a crush on, suddenly appeared! I was so surprised I almost dropped my books, as he stood leaning on his mailbox smiling at me. He asked me a few questions about school, and then invited me to come upstairs, he said that he wanted to show me something. I said no, that I had to get home (*I did!*) my grandmother was expecting me. He tried again to persuade me, but when he saw that he wasn't getting anywhere, to my surprise, he grabbed the stack of books out of my arms, to include my purse, and quickly scurried up the path and into his house.

"What are you doing, give me my books back!" I yelled frantically.

"Come and get them," he teased.

To my horror, I remembered that I had scribbled his name with a heart on one of my binders. It would be so embarrassing if he saw it. He finally persuaded me up the walkway and through the front door, where stairs led to the second floor. Before I knew it, he had lured me into the living room of the small apartment he shared with his family, holding my belongings out of reach. I will never forget the big glass wall mirror of the Veranzano Bridge or the tacky Italian furniture.

He pounced on me at that point, throwing me on the leather couch, forcing my skirt up while he fumbled with his pants. *Was I dreaming? How could this be happening?* I felt humiliated! I had to get out from underneath him somehow! I gathered all of my strength and began to fight with everything I had. After I was able to get my legs under him I pushed him as hard as I could off of me. He stumbled backwards and in a flash I grabbed my purse and books and darted down the stairs and out of the door. I cried the whole way home, going over the dreadful scenario in my mind, not believing that it had happened, trying to understand if it was my fault or not.

When I finally arrived home I was greeted by my anxious grandmother. I tried to tell her what had happened, but I'm not sure she heard me. When she heard the word *"rape"* she started wailing as if she had never heard anything so terrible. I tried to explain that I had fought back and actually I wasn't raped…but she wasn't hearing me as she rocked back and forth in her chair. It never occurred to me to call the police, or to tell anyone else, and after seeing how upset I made my grandmother I decided to try and forget the horrible thing ever happened.

But I couldn't forget. It happened on a Friday, and after spending the weekend in bed, by Monday the thought of facing him in my first class sent me into a panic attack. I told my grandmother that I was sick and took the whole week off from school. I finally gathered enough courage to go back the following week, but I could feel his eyes on me throughout class.

As soon as the bell rang, I ran… out of the door and down the hall, and I kept running…past the security guards and out of the front doors of New Utrecht High School, where I was greeted by the cheerful sounds of birds chirping. I took a deep breath and tried to figure out what I was going to do with the rest of my day. That was the last time I attended my American history class, or the three others that I shared with that horrible boy. That was the end of my high school education and the beginning of my rebellion.

I made a lot of new friends cutting out of class who introduced me to the club scene in New York City where a whole new world opened up to me. My attendance in class was almost non-existent, and if I was in school, I was hanging out in the halls instead of studying.

I remember one instance in particular, when my art teacher grabbed me by my skinny arm, and hauled me into the classroom after catching me sneaking by the open classroom door. I stood at the front of the room, where I faced my empty desk and all the obedient students that were doing what they were supposed to be doing, and I felt ashamed. My teacher scolded me and then asked me what I wanted to do with my life? I just stared at her, my eyes as big as saucers, too afraid to speak. She wrote her daughter's phone number on a scrap of paper and said that she was a photographer for Ford modeling agency in the city and that I should give her a call. I took the scrap of paper and slinked to my desk.

New Utrecht HS, where I rarely attended class. The same high school featured in Welcome Back Kotter Staring John Travolta, a popular TV sitcom from the 70s.

I daydreamed about modeling for about a week, but I was only 14 and I felt like I had all the time in the world to follow up on a modeling career. I guess I was having too much fun that even the prospect of modeling was too serious for me at that point. For the next 2 years, I lived my life on the edge, dating older men and partying a lot. I was only 14, but I lied about my age to get into clubs, and that is when I met a Sicilian gangster that was 15 years older than me. He showered me with the attention that I was lacking from not having a family anymore, and we started dating.

I spent a lot of time sitting in his Cadillac while he did his rounds in Brooklyn, going from one bar café to the next. I would stare out of the window at the dirty streets of Brooklyn and daydream about having a family and someone to care about me. Maybe he would ask me to marry him?

86th street in Bay Ridge, Brooklyn. John Travolta did his famous strut here in the opening scene of Saturday Night Fever.

I was initiated into the dark underworld of the Italian Mafia in Brooklyn in the mid 80s very quickly. Before I realized what was happening, I was in too deep and it became harder and harder for me to walk away. What at first was flattering and made me feel loved, became dark and possessive. When I wasn't with my Mafia boyfriend, he had me followed. One afternoon, after shopping with money he gave me, my friend and I noticed a black Cadillac with tinted windows following us. We giggled about it, and she thought it was cool, but it gave me a sinking feeling in my stomach. The same feeling I always got when something bad was about to happen.

As the weeks went by the threats increased. Pretty soon, I wasn't allowed to go out with my friends at all, he said I had to stay in the house and wait for his call. Whenever he called, I usually had about five minutes to show up outside so he could whizz by and pick me up. One time I refused, and that is when he threatened to hurt my grandmother. He told me he would blow all of the windows out of my house and do terrible things to my poor grandma. With these kinds of threats, I couldn't do anything but listen to him. I felt powerless.

One of the last times I saw him, he came to pick me up after the usual threat that if I wasn't outside in five minutes that he would break granny's neck. I was promptly standing on the curb in four minutes, just to be safe, when I saw him racing down the street, but in a different car than the usual one he drove. He was anxious, and hopped up on cocaine, rambling about this and that.

He made a couple of stops, but as we were heading back to his house, shots rang out, one actually breaking the glass of the back window of his borrowed car! He cursed and swore and he drove like a madman, and when he found an opportunity he booted me out of the door. I walked the rest of the way home in the shadows, looking over my shoulder, worrying that whoever shot at him, would come after me too.

When I returned home my grandmother was frantic. She had been on the phone with my mother demanding that she come and get me. Worried that I wouldn't survive another week in this situation, my mother booked a flight immediately. I didn't share any of my personal business with my grandmother, but she had pieced together bits from reading my diary and listening in on some of my phone calls from the other extension. I could always hear her breathing, and I knew when she listened in. I also censored my diary, because I knew she read it, so the story she was telling everyone was a really watered down version. I am not sure my mother would have come if she knew the real danger she put herself in by showing up to get me.

As we left Brooklyn for the airport, I remember feeling sad, as I waved to my grandmother from the back window of the yellow taxicab. Although New York had become this dangerous place for me, it was still very appealing. My mother was shocked by my transformation after not seeing me for three years.

I tried to live with my mother and follow the rules, but after being in charge of myself for so long it was impossible. You can't set a bird free and then expect it to get back in its cage. I refused to go to high school, I just couldn't relate to kids my own age. I had spent countless nights dancing at Limelight and Palladium in Manhattan and now I was stuck in a trailer park in the middle of nowhere. I agreed to go to beauty school and while out one day searching for a job washing hair, I popped into a hair salon down the road from where I lived, and that is when I met my next boyfriend. He owned a hair salon and he said he needed a receptionist and invited me into his back room to chat. He was a lot better than the boys that were trying to ask me out in vocational school! It took me all of 3 weeks before I moved in with him, or rather moved in *on* him.

I lived with the hairdresser for the next two and a half years, but he never wanted to get serious with me. He said I was too young, and that scared him. He did encourage me to try modeling again and took a bunch of amateur pictures of me. I made an appointment with a modeling agency in Denver in an attempt to do something with my life, and I started working right away, but the jobs weren't as glamorous as I had imagined. Every time I went out on auditions, I would hear the same excuse… *I wasn't in New York and that is where I needed to be to become a professional model.* Although I lost that little slip of paper from my teacher for the photographer daughter, the idea was still in my head. I could go back to New York now that I was older and become a model!

After going on a few more dead-end auditions, my boyfriend suggested that I fly to New York and give it a try. He would pay for my ticket and if I was lucky enough to sign a contract, I would give him a percentage of my earnings for a period of time. Maybe it was a bad deal, but he was really helping me by buying the ticket, so it sounded fair to me.

I didn't want to go to New York on my own, so I invited my brother along for the trip. He hadn't been back to Brooklyn since he left with my Dad and was anxious to see my grandmother again. My father was having a difficult time and I had no contact with him. He was only in Florida for a few months before he was forced to put my brother on a bus to Colorado to live with my mother. I would go to sleep at night and pray that he would contact us and let us know that he was fine. I cried a lot, I even thought that if I became a model maybe he would come back into my life. I could buy him a house and take care of him! I put a lot of pressure on myself.

I honestly didn't give much thought to my Sicilian ex-boyfriend. I figured that over two years had passed and he would have forgotten all about me, when I was with him, I was underage, and he could get in trouble. I was older and wiser now (*but still underage!*) and realized I had rights and I shouldn't be afraid to visit the place where I was born, the place where most of my family lived, and maybe the place that held some kind of future for me. So fueled by these thoughts, my brother and I boarded a flight to New York and took a taxi back to Brooklyn.

We arrived on a Saturday, and we planned on staying until Wednesday. On Monday, we would take the train into Manhattan and visit Ford Modeling Agency.

5th Avenue NYC.

I seemed to be able to come and go without any problem that weekend. We had a great time and I was reminded of why I loved

Brooklyn so much.

On Monday, we took the train to Manhattan. As we approached the little inconspicuous brownstone building, I realized I should probably be going in alone, so I asked my brother to wait outside. I went up to the front door and quickly entered before I lost my nerve. The small reception area was plastered with the faces of models I recognized from magazines, and before I could register any of it, I was ushered into another small office by a rather stern-looking woman. She sat behind her desk and scrutinized my face for five minutes, *why is she frowning?*

She asked me to stand and walk and some of my confidence returned as I glided back and forth across the room attemping my version of a supermodel walk.

"*Sit.*" She firmly commanded.

I sat. And that's when she gave me the bad news. I was the right height, but, she didn't think I had the right look for Ford and I wouldn't do very well against their other models. I felt deflated. I thanked her for her time, and because I didn't want her to see me upset, I made my escape. To make matters worse, as I was leaving, I brushed shoulders with one of their models.
My brother was anxiously waiting for me, leaning up against a car and he had not failed to notice the model that went in before I came out and I could see he was impressed. I quickly told him my version of the events, that I was not pretty, or good enough for Ford.

We slumped back to the train station. On the way, I received a random whistle from a passing car, typical in New York, and my brother, in attempt to lift my spirits, said it didn't matter what Ford thought, their models all looked like dorks anyway. I laugh to myself when I think of that, because it was kind of the right thing to say. After my crushing experience, I was ready to go back to Colorado and face my fate. I would have to come up with another plan to make it big. Of course, we couldn't escape without drama, and on our last night in Brooklyn, there was an unexpected knock on the front door.

My brother and I peered cautiously through the curtains of the upstairs window, and to my horror, I saw the familiar silhouette of the person I had run from two years before. *Oh my God, it was him, why did I think I could come back so easily?* He was double parked yelling my name in the street. He wanted to see me, but my grandmother insisted that I didn't live there anymore. She told him to go away or she would call the police, as my poor brother paced back and forth looking extremely worried. Luckily, nothing happened, and the Sicilian went away, although I spent that last night in Brooklyn sleeping with one eye open.

Chapter 3

Dreams shattered, time to move on!

Reluctantly, I returned to Colorado and spent the next year working dead-end modeling jobs. In that time, my mother, her husband, and my sister moved to Texas. I stayed with my hairdresser boyfriend, but it was basically a relationship going nowhere. I knew that I didn't have a future with him, problem was, I didn't have anywhere else to go. He had recently made some bad gambling deals and his hair salon was going under. We lived in a rundown apartment in Aurora, and my brother lived above us, in an (*even more*) rundown apartment.

Colfax Avenue, Denver Colorado in the 80s.

My dad showed up at one point, and he lived upstairs with my brother for a short time. I was so happy to have my dad close, and from then on he was back in my life more consistently. My dad always apologized for not being able to take care of me. I knew how much he loved me, but the hand that life had dealt him was a bad one.

In the last 6 years, my father had drifted in and out of mental hospitals, he was even rescued from jumping off of a bridge! I remember when I accidently found his suicide note that he wasn't able to leave because his plan was sabotaged, hidden inside his duffle bag. I cried my eyes out at the thought that he felt so alone that he wanted to end everything. Didn't he know I was alone too? If we just helped each other everything would be okay.

My dad decided to get help from the Veteran system, so he moved to Palo Alto, California and was admitted into the Veterans Hospital. I can't tell you how much better I slept at night knowing that my dad was safe. My father had spent 15 years in the military with a tour in Vietnam that won him a bronze star and a lot of mental problems. His job was particularly brutal, called *"tunnel rat,"* because he would go down into the tunnels of the Vietcong, and using special dogs, he would capture them! It was a job that left my father with PTSD, which, as I mentioned earlier, surfaced in full force with the trauma of the divorce from my mother. My father needed help and he was finally going to get it!

In the fall of 1990, I met my first husband while working a job bagging groceries at an Air Force base commissary. He came from a family of officers, so to me, his life was a privileged one. He had a nice house and a nice car and he was graduating from high school, working at the commissary to make extra money. His family was kind to me and took me in like I was one of their own. We all sat around the dinner table in the evening like a real family and talked about our day. My life became a whirlwind of planning, and before I knew it I was married to a Marine Corps recruit and my first son was born. We were stationed in Memphis, Tennessee first, and then Jacksonville, North Carolina, where my second son was born, a couple of years later.

I did my best to construct the life I never had growing up. I cooked and I cleaned and I took care of my kids as a stay at home mom. With my support, my husband excelled in his career, receiving meritorious promotions left and right. It's pretty normal for Marines to deploy, but when he volunteered to join Special Forces for a more dangerous job that had him deployed most of the time, the marriage began to crumble. I was left alone in a strange place with no money and two babies. I was used to this kind of lifestyle, being a military brat myself, but it's a lot harder when you have only yourself to depend on. My dad was worried about me, so he packed up his life, and came to stay close by to help me take care of the boys after my husband's first deployment.

He was doing much better financially, and mentally he was on medication for his PTSD, which also helped him function normally. We made up for all of the lost years when I was a teenager and we had long conversations about life. My loyalty to my dad was always really strong, my love for him couldn't be measured, except for the love I had for my children. I was surrounded by love for the first time in my life.

In the mid-80s, when my mother remarried, there was a court order for my dad to pay child support for my sister, even though he had full custody of both me and my brother. Regardless, my father religiously sent money to my sister, not through the court system, but directly to her. Money order after money order, for years and years, and a big lump sum of $10,000 when Social Security was rewarded to her because of my dad's illness. There is a reason I am writing this, and I will return to it later.

When my husband came home from deployment he was a changed person. He had acquired some bad habits on the ship, that I won't go into, as well as battle scars from being in a war zone for part of his six-month deployment. With the mounting money problems, the stress of taking care of two kids on my own, and the emotional detachment we both felt for each other, the marriage was on a downward spiral. We blamed our problems on everyone else and decided a change of scenery might be the answer. It was time to move anyway, but in the Marine Corps duty stations are limited. We decided on Okinawa, Japan. It was an exotic tropical island in the South Pacific, so why not? I was tired of living in North Carolina and I wanted some excitement in my life. So we sold our house, packed everything up, and moved to the other side of the world!

Chapter 4

Japan

I fell in love with the beauty of Japan instantly. We were surrounded by nature and the sparkling blue-green sea on one side of the island, and the majestic Pacific on the other. We were approaching springtime and I was thrilled!

Unfortunately, my bubble of happiness burst fairly quickly when my husband began mentally abusing me and the kids, something that he had never done before. He used intimidation tactics and called me terrible names, he even kicked me out of the house, which was devastating as I was on an island on the other side of the planet from anyone that cared about me. I remember a frantic call to my father telling him the awful situation I was in. He wasn't thrilled about me moving so far away, but he understood that it was military life, that you moved, and then you moved back. He basically told me to suck it up and make the best of it, so I tried.

In the middle of all this, my husband deployed for a few months again, leaving me alone in Okinawa, but this time I had a heavy heart and a desire to get the heck out of my bad situation. I guess with what I learned in my life growing up, when things got bad, you just got out, *and I wanted out!*

Walking around a botanical garden one afternoon, a talent scout from Elite Tokyo Modeling Agency approached me. Wow, it seemed like the universe was showing me an open door, and I didn't hesitate to walk through it! When my husband came home, I told him that I wanted to go to Tokyo to become a model. The problem was the boys, I couldn't take them with me, and he couldn't watch them. I made the painstaking decision to send them back to America for a short time so I could work and save money. Saying goodbye to my children was unbearble. They were so little and they needed me! I didn't have a future without modeling and this was a huge opportunity for me. I would have to make a big sacrifice, but in the end, I tried to focus on the rewards of having my own life without being abused mentally and sexually, something that also began after my husband returned from his first deployment. My inlaws were wonderful. My mother-in-law quit her job as a full time nurse to care for her grandkids, and she embraced the opportunity to be close to them, especially after a recent tear-filled goodbye, when we left for Japan.

I worked in Tokyo for about 4 months and saved up a small amount to start over. I had long conversations with my dad and we decided that me and the boys would move to Colorado and live with him. I was supposed to continue working in Tokyo, but I couldn't live with the heartache of being so far away from my children. The phone calls weren't enough. I took a trip back to Okinawa once a month, but it didn't help my marriage, if anything, it hurt it. We both had been unfaithful to each other and I didn't have the skills to deal with any of it, it just made me want to run as far away as I could.

My husband's anger problems had accelerated, and he was getting into trouble at work. One afternoon, I decided enough was enough, and I packed up my bags and went to Virginia to be with my sons.

It was February of 1999, and I spent the next four months living with my husband's parents while my husband stayed in Okinawa on his own. The kids were in the middle of the school year and I didn't want to disrupt their lives again. I was so damaged by my parents divorce, that the last thing I ever wanted to do was to put my children through the same thing...but...*my husband was not a man of high caliber like my father was,* I wish someone would have explained that to me at the time. I just wanted a good life for my kids, they were my world and I wanted to make it a happy place. I let everyone know that I wanted a divorce. There was crying, there was screaming, there was a lot of theatrics, and it was all from adults!

I had a bulldozer of guilt thrown on me and the final straw was when I was forced to join a conference call with my husband and his parents, and this time they were *all* crying!

"My god! Okay! I will go back!"

There were a lot of promises that were made and intentions to change, and I wanted to believe him, so I did. I had to try one more time, for the boys. I didn't want them to grow up like I did and I didn't have the education to make enough money to raise them on my own. Okinawa was so beautiful and I had barely seen any of it.

Singing karaoke in Tokyo 1998.

He seemed sorry, so I reluctantly returned to Japan and I tried as hard as I could to be happy. We actually spent a decent year and a half exploring the island and trying to be a family, but the ghosts from the past still lurked in the shadows and came out to haunt us now and then. There were trust issues and anger issues, and I was still hurt from being mistreated, but we managed to somehow provide a loving home for Nick and Tony.

Chapter 5

Back to Colorado

When the tour in Okinawa came to a close, my husband made the difficult decision not to reenlist. He blamed a lot of our problems on the military and he always wanted to be an air traffic controller for the FAA. In the transition period, while looking for a job, we decided to live with his parents in Virginia. We were only there for a short time before he received an acceptance letter from Denver Center, one of the biggest, most important airports in the nation. We were going back to Colorado!

We found a new place in a nice area, near the facility that my husband would be training at, and life seemed to be …okay. I wasn't happy, but I wasn't as miserable as I had been. I realized my husband was a lot easier to deal with as long as he got his way. I made sure that the kids stayed quiet and the house was clean and he had home cooked meals on the table any time he wanted to eat. He was withdrawn and stressed because of his new career and the difficulties that come with being an air traffic controller, but I tried to be supportive!

While I was in Japan, I was only able to see my father one time, and that was in May of 1999, when I was living in Virginia, waiting for school to be let out. In the meantime, he had met a wonderful lady and they had purchased an RV together. Their plan was to travel to National parks around the country and enjoy retirement. It was the perfect lifestyle for my dad, he loved traveling and seeing new places. I couldn't wait to see my father happy!

It was April of 2002, just after Easter, and my dad and Joanie were planning to drive from Las Vegas to Colorado to see us. During that time, the majority of my thoughts were on making everything perfect for his visit. He had been so concerned for me when I was in Japan, and he was glad that I was trying to make my marriage work despite the problems that we had buried. I really wanted to show my father that I was fine, and that his grandsons were fine too! Unfortunately, I never got that chance.

Chapter 6

Tragedy strikes

It was the morning of April 2, and my father called to let me know that he was having something sent to him at my address. I missed his call, because I was busy cleaning, preparing for his arrival the next day. I smiled to myself as I listened to his message. I imagined seeing my dad and hugging him again. With that thought, I decided to take a nap. I had been up since 6 am, and I felt exhausted.

An hour later, I was startled awake by the landline. I checked the caller ID, and it said, *Las Vegas Police Department.* My heart began to race. I answered the phone, and it was Joanie, my Dad's girlfriend. She was crying hysterically, saying she was so sorry!

"Whats wrong?"

"It's your dad...he's dead..."

But what she was saying just didn't register!

"What? What? What are you talking about?"

She tried to explain to me what had happened, but I couldn't understand. I was in shock. I told her to make sure, that he can't be dead, I just heard him on the answering machine, she must be wrong!

But it was true. On the way to see me they pulled into an RV park in Nevada, and as my Dad was parking, his RV hit the side of another RV, and the owner was *really* mad. So angry that he came storming out of his RV screaming and threatening to call the police. This was the worst thing he could have said! My father was living with a secret, and it was about to be revealed. He had been driving without a license for a couple of years, because when his old license expired, he simply couldn't renew it because of my mother's court order. The child support, and the demon behind it, reared its ugly head to haunt him one more time, and ultimately, ended his life. He owed back child support of over $20,000... There was no record of the money he sent to my sister, because he didn't go through the court system, too afraid my *stepfather* would take the money. My father panicked. A psychic told me months later that my dad was like a pressure cooker ready to explode, and it just took that one incident to send him over the edge.

The thought of jail was too much for him. He had been a POW in Vietnam, and wore bracelets for the forgotten Vets left behind. He would rather die with dignity than be imprisoned, so he calmly excused himself, boarded his RV, went to the back bedroom where he kept his rifle, the same model he used in Vietnam, and he shot himself in the chest. A tragic end, to a remarkable man. The days, weeks, months, and years that followed, are all a blurry, painful memory. It took me two years to be able to even function normally again. Unfortunately, during that time, the tragedy didn't help my marriage. After a month, my husband expected me to be back to my old self, and I wasn't. I wanted to die too. The only thing that was keeping me alive was my children. I would have followed my father if they weren't there. I know that.

Ft. Logan Cemetary. Denver, Colorado. RIP Dad.

Chapter 7

From bad to worse

One year melted into the next with no distinction in between. I was growing more and more discontent with my life with each passing day. My husband and I had almost nothing in common anymore, and his interests kept him away from home most of the time. I tried to be a good sport and play along, but I was growing weary in my life. I don't know if it was because of the way that my father had died, but every time I looked at my husband's guns I felt like something bad was going to happen, and my intuition proved to be unfortunately, correct. Something bad did happen.

Late one September evening as I was cleaning up the dinner dishes, I casually peered out of the kitchen window as the sun was going down, and to my horror, I noticed flames billowing up from the top of the mountain of rocks behind our house. One of the pines was on fire! The fire department came quickly and put the fire out, but they informed us that there were remnants of a homemade explosive present, and they would have to call Homeland Security.

My oldest son was questioned, and was even made to show his Facebook account. There were 4 other teenagers involved, but luckily Nick wasn't one of them. The boys were just taking advantage of the empty lot behind our house to explode fireworks. We were all disturbed this had happened, but I honestly don't know what had gotten into my husband. He said that he had to protect his land so he gathered all of his weapons and called a former Marine friend over to help him guard the house the following night. I felt that it was a completely ridiculous idea, as the trespassers were just a bunch of kids, not the Taliban. I made dinner and put the kids to bed at around 10, while my husband and his friend played cards, accompanied by glasses of whiskey and a lot of macho talk that I didn't have any interest in listening to.

I busied myself making up the couch, because after a few drinks I knew his friend would not be going anywhere that night. I had my suspicions that he had arrived drunk in the first place! So many alarms were going off in my head and I really wanted to voice my concerns, but it seemed that my opinion didn't seem to matter anymore. Whether it was my thoughts on not purchasing expensive items, to my view on guns, to my view on hunting. I was in such an unsettling place inside myself. I hated the way I felt. I had no control over the chaos around me.

A shout from the dining room startled me out of my thoughts, apparently they heard something in the back of the house, or thought they heard something.

Before I realized what was happening, my husband was shouting at me to stay in the house as he quickly ran out of the back door with his loaded shotgun. His friend ran past me out of the front door with another loaded gun.
Oh my god. What if there are kids out there? This was not good. I had to do something!!

That's when two shots rang out in succession. *Pop. Pop.* I ran to the back door where my husband had disappeared only moments earlier, and as I was turning the handle, his friend ran in through the front door, yelling.

"Call the police, I just shot him !!!"

I just stood there frozen with my mouth hanging open.

"You did WHAT?"

The reality of what happened slowly dawned on me and somehow I managed to stop my shaking hand long enough to dial 911 as I raced to where he was laying. It was hard to form a coherent sentence, but I informed the operator that my husband had been shot and to send an ambulance! He was lying on his stomach on the ground with blood pouring out of his upper leg area. His friend was there next to me moments later and he attempted to compress the wound with kitchen towels until help could arrive.

In less than 5 minutes, the ambulance arrived, and police and snipers surrounded the house. Because of my frantic phone call they didn't know what kind of situation they would be confronting and were taking precautionary measures. My husband was taken to the local hospital, and then medevaced down the mountain by helicopter. The detective questioned me and he was able to access what had happened fairly quickly and arrested the friend, who in his drunken stupor mistook my husband for an intruder and shot him twice. None of this was my fault, but I felt responsible. You just don't act like this when you have kids in the house!! You don't drink and handle guns! It's a fatal mixture! I was so happy when the detective and deputy seized all of his guns.

A social worker came to sit with me while I waited for my husband's parents to arrive. We sat in silence for three hours, as I kept going over the incident in my mind, still not believing it had happened. My husband was extremely lucky. He was shot with a .44 magnum and doctors said that he should have died, or been paralyzed, but thankfully the bullet had missed vital areas and besides walking with a slight limp, he recovered in a couple of months after spending some time in the hospital.

While in the hospital, I had long talks with him and there were a lot of promises that he would stop drinking. I threw away all the alcohol in the house, but unfortunately, his promise to stop drinking faded after two months and he was back to drinking again. Everyone in town knew what had happened and the yellow police tape that surrounded the crime scene for the first week after the incident didn't help matters. I didn't like the attention, or the assumptions. I was a victim of circumstance and I didn't want to be a victim of anything!

Bad choices were made that affected myself, and the lives of my children and I had to make a change or I was going to continue to live like this. I didn't know how, as it seemed something that was impossible to accomplish, but I was going to leave him!

Trying to restart my modeling career in 2008.

It was the summer of 2008, when I wrote to one of my old contacts in Japan to see if he could find me job. It had been 10 years, but Japan was the only place I knew of where I could make enough money to start over. I was responsible for paying all of our bills and I knew we were in over our heads. There was no way that my husband would be able to maintain me with all of the bills we had accumulated. I tried to pay everything on time, but I was losing control. The stress was getting to be too much for me. I had a few panic attacks and made the stupid decision to medicate myself with alcohol. I felt ashamed of my life. I imagined what my father would think. He wouldn't want me to be this way. A couple of drinking episodes had ended with me blacking out, which was very scary! I guess that is what brought me to the bottom of my closet on New Year's Eve, and my wish for a way out.

Chapter 8

Leo

My first reply to Leo was in Italian and it was very brief. I liked the fact that he mentioned that he had just spent some time in Colorado just a few months before, *is that why he felt so familiar to me?* I told him I found it hard to imagine an eccentric character like him hanging out around here.

He made me feel beautiful and smart and he said to me all the things that I ached to hear. He was the only person that told me that I needed to stop drinking. He could see I had a problem, even from so far away. Looking back on the way everything transpired, I am not sure I would have done anything differently. I had to make tough decisions to change my life. I had tried over and over to make a life with my husband, but we were on two different paths. I was 37 years old and I felt I had spent most of my younger years having to face one tragedy after another.

My oldest son had matured quite a bit, and from 2007, I barely saw him. He had a girlfriend and a job and a whole life away from home. Kids understand and I couldn't shield him from all of the problems. When he told me he wanted to join the Marine Corps and be an air traffic controller like his father, I had mixed feelings. With all the problems that *that* career field had given us, I wasn't keen on the idea at first, but it would be an excellent income if he could manage the stress of the job without depending on alcohol to unwind. He was almost 18 years old, he was a man now, and he wanted to make a life for himself. I felt so proud of him.

My youngest son was almost 16 and still had another 2 years of high school. He would suffer the most in the breakup of my marriage. I tried to take things day by day, and I kept Leo a secret at first. I remembered what happened the last time I tried to leave and I didn't want to go through that again. I had enough guilt trips thrown on me in my life. I had spent 17 years raising two boys virtually on my own and in those years I had spent most of them unhappy. The timing wasn't perfect, but you can't plan everything.

Leo had a lot of bad luck in his life too. He had just returned to Italy after living many years abroad after going through a traumatic experience. In 2007, before his trip to America, his wife took away his infant son in the wee hours of the morning and at the same time she turned him into the Norwegian Secret Service. After his separation and eventual divorce, he felt he needed to escape all of the heartache, so for 3 months he traveled across America, and spent most of his time in Colorado, just down the canyon from where I lived. Fate didn't let us meet each other then, but he recalled that during that trip, he would look up at the mountains and feel my presence there. I thought that was so magical, because I actually had this nagging feeling during that time, that he was close too.

Even with all the divine connections, a part of me was in denial and since none of it would be easy, I got cold feet quite a bit at the thought of meeting each other. I think in the back of my mind I knew that once I met him there would be no going back, he would be with me forever. *But why did the timing have to be so inconvenient?*

Leo bought a ticket to come to America, but I chickened out at the last minute and told him to cancel it. I even tried to stop talking to him and changed my phone number, but I failed miserably. He had captured my heart, and going just a few hours without speaking to him was *torture*!

I mentioned earlier that I had contacted someone that I knew from Japan to find me a modeling job, and to my surprise, he found me a job in Okinawa! It wasn't exactly the kind of modeling job I liked, but it was paying a lot of money and it would help me with my future plans to leave my marriage. The job would be helping to organize a reggae concert with all the top names in the business. They needed organizers that looked appealing and I jumped at the chance and agreed to take the job. I would leave in June and spend 10 days in Okinawa.

April 2009.

In the meantime, I spoke to Leo daily, living a double life. I can't say this made me feel very good about myself. My husband agreed to let me go to Japan because it would be a lot of money that he thought could help with our financial situation. I was pretty depressed after canceling Leo's trip to America, I had to find another way to see him! I needed to know for sure if what we had was real.

That's when I decided to take a short trip to Rome and covered up the trip with lies. Maybe in the back of my mind I hoped that I wouldn't love him and I could just put an end to this whole idea of a relationship with a man on the other side of the world. I couldn't see how it could work, anyway. I was stuck where I was until my youngest son was at least off to college. The job in Japan might give me the opportunity to leave and find an apartment, but I was still stuck. I fantasized that I could get an apartment of my own with Tony and that Leo could come and visit us freely, and we could go to Italy to visit him. Of course, life hardly ever goes the way you daydream, or even the way you plan.

Chapter 9

Rome

My feelings for Leo were so overwhelming I felt myself making decisions like I was on autopilot. I *had* to meet him, so I planned a short trip in April 2009. As I sat in my seat, gazing out of the window of the airplane on its way to Rome, life couldn't seem more surreal. I felt like I was being catapulted into a magical world and I didn't know what to expect. I spent much of the flight daydreaming, picturing how it would be to finally be close to each other.

Throughout my life, I have had flashbacks of another time, where I can see myself riding a horse in a beautiful meadow and a castle can be seen in the distance. I have always had this terrible fear of being thrown off of a horse, so I never understood the horse vision, until now. A man was riding next to me, he had a sword by his side and he was dressed as a knight. I realized sitting on the plane, on my way to a far off land, that that man was Leo! I could see in another vision the same scene, except this time the man was distraught, weeping over me. I was dead, blood pouring from my head after being thrown from my horse. It felt as if I had opened a door to another world with a hidden key and I was finally able to see the meaning of this reoccurring past life vision.

First time meeting Leo in Rome in April 2009.

Rooftop view of the Vatican area.

The Roman Forum.

I landed in Rome, but Leo wasn't there to meet me at the airport because we had decided that I would take a taxi and pick him up on the way to my hotel. It wasn't really the way that I pictured our first encounter to be, but I was so excited to meet him, I didn't care if it wasn't what I had imagined. Leo had a girlfriend in Rome so he was afraid to meet me at his flat, and because I was not really a person who should be judging anyone, I kept my mouth shut about it. From what I could tell from what he told me, she was just someone that kept him company since returning to Italy in 2008. I figured that if he was in love with her he wouldn't be talking to me. I still hoped that maybe we could keep our relationship casual, and Leo having a girlfriend helped that. We would have to be a little bit careful though, so it made everything...*exciting!*

On my way to Leo in the taxi, I thought back to our many conversations. *Be still my beating heart!* I checked and rechecked myself in my little makeup mirror and made small talk with the taxi driver as we edged closer to San Giovanni. We passed the Ancient Ruins of Rome, and then there was the Colisseum! I had been to Rome plenty of times as a tourist, but never like this. I was about to meet the man of my dreams... *literally.* I told the driver we would be making one stop, and as he pulled up to the address, *I saw him.* He spotted the taxi and put his hand up, and then smoothly slid in next to me. When Leo turned to me, and took my hand...I felt the foundation of my soul tremble and awaken...and when he kissed me, I knew that my search for him was over.

We arrived at the hotel too quickly, I almost wished there were more time, everything was happening really fast. I took a few deep breaths and exited the taxi as Leo held the door open for me and helped me with my bags. I knew what he looked like from all the months of talking on Skype and his interviews that I watched on Youtube, but I thought he looked better in person.

He sneaked a couple of peaks at me on the way to the elevators, and as soon as we opened the door to my room we embraced and started kissing. He had me pressed up against the door of the bathroom, and when I tried to escape to freshen up after the long flight, he wouldn't let me go.

I squirmed out of his embrace and ran into the bathroom for a few moments to freshen up, but two minutes later he was behind me panting heavily. I finally gave in to my desire and let myself go. It began to thunderstorm, and lightning put even more electricity into the air than there already was. We spent the rest of the afternoon lost in another place, in another time, and I experienced ecstasy like I had never known.

Chapter 10

Academy of the Illuminati

I think I could have stayed in bed with Leo until the next day, but he had an interview scheduled that evening with Panorama, a weekly Italian-language news magazine published in Italy, and he invited me to come along. I was exhausted, but I didn't want to miss anything, so I freshened up and we took off for the center of Rome, to the office where the interview was being held. The interview was about the new movie Angels and Demons, that was just released in the cinemas in Italy.

I chose a pretty spring dress in a bright color in hopes that it would help me to wake up a little bit, but I should've had a coffee because on the way I felt myself dozing off a few times. The taxi pulled up to an impressive building, and we got out quickly, greeted by the doorman who looked Leo's name up in the registry. The interviewer, Giacomo Amadori, was waiting for Leo in Piergiorgio Bassi's office, someone that Leo mentions a few times in his *Confession's* series. He is the Vice President of the Academy of the Illuminati and a very compelling character. When Leo introduced me in a grandiose way, as if I were a princess, I laughed to myself and thought, *This was going to be an interesting 5 days!*

Leo went off with Piergiorgio and Giacomo to conduct his interview, and I was led to a small room by the secretary of Mr. Bassi. I definitely felt like I was in Italy, with the marble floors and fashionable décor, and I wondered how long I would have to wait.

There was an open window across from me, and the cool evening air sent a shiver up my spine. I should've worn a sweater, but I think if it wasn't for that cool breeze, I might have fallen asleep. I watched the old fashioned clock sitting on a little mahogany side table next to the sofa...tick tock-one hour...tick tock-two hours....*I had to use the bathroom!*

I was beginning to wonder if they had forgotten about me, because besides the ticking of the clock, I hadn't heard a sound from anywhere inside the building. I thought that if another hour went by maybe I would have to escape out of the open window. After a few more minutes passed, I got up to stretch my legs, and walked over to the window, just to imagine if it were possible for me to make an escape in such a manner. At that moment, the door flew open, and Leo and Piergiorgio appeared. I was so relieved!

We spent some time saying goodbye, but when we were finally free we bolted out of the door and ran towards the train. Torrents of rain assaulted us and we didn't have an umbrella, so by the time we arrived to the street of my hotel, we were soaked. We popped into a restaurant on the corner for dinner, and spent the next few hours enjoying each other's company. It seemed like we had been rushing through the whole day, but now, finally, we could relax.

I was living on borrowed time, so I tried to take advantage of every moment I had with Leo. I felt like a kid, exploring secret corridors and alleys, where the ancient magic of Rome could be felt around every corner. I never experienced such great food, such great wine, and such intriguing conversation. This was going to be hard to let go of, I was already being pulled in, and there wasn't anything I could do to stop it! On my last day, Leo took me to meet his family in the mountains outside of Rome.

Leo's mother poured tea and cut a homemade apple cake, as we sat in the living room of the rustic Italian villa in the middle of the countryside. Leo's father looked at me intently and asked me a load of questions about my time in Japan. I was going back there soon, as I had mentioned my job in the summer, and he was very interested in hearing all of the details. When we said goodbye, I felt that it was more like a hello...because I could feel I would be returning soon.

To my despair, my magical adventure with the man that I had been searching my whole life for had come to an end, and it was time for me to leave. I think I cried the whole taxi ride to the airport, and I didn't stop until I was somewhere over Novia Scotia. I watched the inflight map on the little screen in my seat and felt my heart break as the miles accumulated, and then...we were worlds apart again. *Oh boy. This wasn't what I imagined it would be. This was intense!* I tried to think about my kids, and how excited they would be to see me and that helped to ease the pain a little. I bought them presents in Rome and I was excited to see them and give them out.

I tried to go back to living a normal life, but I was having a lot of problems. I felt myself becoming jealous of Leo's girlfriend, although I tried to keep those feelings to myself. He was also jealous of the time I spent with my husband, and pushed me to go forward with divorce plans.

I told him I needed money first, and I would have to focus on this job I had coming up in Japan, because it was basically my only way out. Leo had gone through a bitter divorce himself, and after the sale of his house in Norway, his money was tied up in court proceedings until 2010. He was basically broke, so he couldn't really help me financially, and I didn't expect him to. I wasn't a gold digger. I had to find a way to meet him again!

The idea to have Leo accompany me to Japan came spontaneously one afternoon in May 2009. It had been a month since we had spent our 5 days together in Rome, and all I could think about was how we could be together again. I arranged to meet Leo in Tokyo for 8 days before my 10 days in Okinawa. My plane ticket from the company sponsoring the concert hadn't been sent yet, so I quickly arranged to have two flights, one to Tokyo, and than a second flight to Okinawa. It cost the same amount, so it wasn't a problem for them. Leo had some connections in Tokyo and was very keen on taking the trip with me. He was as anxious to see me again, as I was to see him. I floated through my days dreaming of when he would hold me again.

I was still drinking quite a bit, maybe even more after returning from Rome. It became hard to get through each day, take care of my family, and pretend everything was normal when it was so far from it. My husband should have realized that I just wasn't there anymore. *How could he not know there was someone else?* Well, if he didn't know then, it was confirmed to him the night before I left for Japan.

Chapter 11

Tokyo

I made a very bad decision to have dinner and drinks with my husband and some aquaintances the night before my scheduled flight from Denver to Seattle, and then Tokyo, and if I could take back that night, I would. I was in the company of people I didn't like, and to deal with it, I drank a little more. Everyone was excited about my trip to Japan, and it was the talk around the table at dinner. By the time I made it back to my house it was late, and I would have to wake up early the next morning. I collapsed in bed and basically passed out.

A short time later, I was startled awake by my husband yelling. I couldn't remember how I got into bed, I didn't know how I ended up naked, and worst of all, my husband was yelling obsenities and waving my cell phone at me! He said he was trying to set my alarm for the morning, saw I had a message, and decided to listen to it. It was Leo, and of course anything that Leo said would incriminate me. I was drunk and I guess all the built up emotions over the previous months exploded. He held the phone over my head so I couldn't reach it and accused me of everything I was guilty of doing. I told him that he was right. I had warned him so many times this would happen, what did he expect? Leo didn't mention Japan in the message, so I was basically able to (*lie*) my way out of most of what was said, although recalling it is hazy. We went to bed angry, we woke up angry, and he took me to the airport angry. He still let me go though, despite what he had heard the night before. He knew there was another man and yet he let me leave.

We said our good-byes and I was relieved to see him walk away. I was set free, like a butterfly escaping a glass jar. We didn't talk about Leo again and when I called him from Seattle I told him that we should try harder to make our marriage better, that the alcohol was ruining everything. It was my last attempt, and I obviously didn't believe on following through with the promises because I was off to be with another man. I didn't want to be this person I was turning into.

I thought a lot on the flight to Japan, and I had many hours to think. You are given one life, if you make choices when you are young and then change as you get older, where is the crime in that? It's wrong to be dishonest, but I felt that I was so trapped that I had to lie! I tried to leave him before and failed miserably. I had tried and tried again and there was nothing I could do to make things better. He didn't want to change, no matter how many times I threatened to leave. I didn't want to make any more threats. I was happy with Leo, and I deserved happiness.

I had confessed to both of my kids about Leo. I knew that when I got back from Japan, and if I still felt the same way about him, that I would have to have a plan. This job in Okinawa had to work out! It was my only way out. So I focused all of my energy on those thoughts, as I drifted off to sleep, somewhere over the Pacific.

∞∞∞

Several hours later, I stirred in my seat and awoke, greeted by Mt Fuji peeking through misty clouds. I was on the other side of the world now, far away from all of the problems at home. I wished I could absorb the vast green of the landscape, maybe it could heal my heart. The air is different in Japan, and I could feel the warm humidity even on the airplane. It was wonderful! I couldn't wait to show Leo all of my favorite parts of Tokyo, like he did for me, when we were in Rome together.

So, besides a slight hangover, I made it to Japan in one piece. Leo arrived late on a different flight, which allowed me to go quickly to the hotel, drop off my bags, and freshen up, before I raced back to the airport to meet him. I paced back and force waiting to see his familiar silhouette appear, and when I spotted him, my heart skipped a beat. I couldn't believe we were in Japan together. It was like a dream come true!

We embraced and kissed each other deeply, as lovers who have been separated for months do. When I was close to him I just felt better, no matter what chaos was going on around me. My place was in his arms again. I couldn't deny it any longer. I vowed to enjoy every moment we spent together as if they were our last. We boarded the bus to the hotel I chose close to the airport. Leo was getting a real kick out of Japan, bowing a lot, and I thought that was so funny.

We spent the first couple of days getting acquainted again. Leo had scheduled an interview with a journalist in Tokyo, and we would be meeting him on Monday. To get to the city center it would take 2.5 hours by train, so my hotel wasn't the best choice for that reason, but the hours seemed to fly by when we were together, even on a smoke filled train bound for Tokyo. In the 10 years that passed since living in Tokyo, I forgot a lot of my navigation skills, and we got lost more than once.

We managed to make it to our destination and met Benjamin Fulford on the corner of a busy side street in Shinjuku. We said our hellos, and Leo commenced with his interview. The place chosen for the interview was a karaoke room which I found rather funny, and I amused myself by thumbing through the books of songs. I didn't have much of an opinion about Benjamin at that time. He seemed like a pleasant, rather eccentric guy, and I figured this type of character was normal for Leo to meet.

Our first meeting with Benjamin Fulford outside a karaoke place in Tokyo April 2009.

The first interview in a karoke room near Ueno park.

Sushi at Benjamin's favorite spot. I tripped over a bucket of fish heads in the bathroom of the place.

Leo loved Tokyo!

At Benjamin Fulford's house, Leo is pointing to a Chinese Freemasonry picture Ben had hung on his wall. Not sure what the green creature was, it seemed a lot of strange organic life thrived in Benjamin's house, especially in his bathroom!

Leo meeting Princess Kaorou Nakamaru for the first time in Tokyo April 2009.

We met Benjamin for three separate interviews, which all seemed very productive, and in the end, those interviews wound up being two best selling books in Japan. Leo signed a book deal during one of the meetings, so the 8 days in Tokyo turned out well. I also had the pleasure of meeting Princess Kaoru Nakamaru, someone Leo writes about a lot in his *Confession's* series. They conducted their interview behind closed doors that was later published on Youtube.

We spent our last day together in Japan at Tokyo Disneyland, and it took hours by train to get there. We had a wonderful time skipping around the park, riding the Pirates of the Carribean ride and laughing a lot. I was able to forget some of my troubles that day, which was really good for me. I needed to relax as much as possible because when Leo left Tokyo, I would have to continue on to Okinawa, in hopes that the job that was waiting for me would give me the opportunity to change my life when I got back to America.

Tokyo Disneyland.

There were phone calls to our partners daily, and when Leo spoke to his girlfriend in Rome, it seemed like he was still holding on to his relationship with her, and since I didn't know what the future would hold, I kept my mouth shut. He never said anything to me when I spoke to my husband, and doubt began to creep in as to what we had together. Maybe I exaggerated everything in my mind and it was just going to be a casual fling that would end after Japan? He was able to sign a book contract and I was happy about that. A divorce would be messy and I am sure he would want to stay far away. It was a lot of strange emotions to wrestle with and when Leo's trip to Tokyo came to a close, I was distraught.

The morning that he left, my heart felt like it would break in two. I swallowed hard, as I waved goodbye, attempting a brave smile. From the curb, as I sadly watched him depart on a shuttle for the airport, from the hotel we had spent so many wonderful days and nights together. I let out a gasp as the bus disappeared into traffic and then the tears came, flowing down my face like two rivers. *When would I see him again? Would I see him again?* I was frightened. The warm humid breeze quickly dried my tears as I took a couple of deep breaths. Leo was gone, and I was alone in Japan.

Chapter 12

Okinawa

I returned to the hotel room and packed my bags, and in less than an hour I was on a shuttle bound for Haneda, the airport that serviced local flights in and around Japan and Okinawa. Leo left the t-shirt he had slept in the night before, and I could still smell him on it. I inhaled deeply, but it sent me into a crying fit, ruining my makeup. In the end, I decided my tears weren't going to stop easily that day, so I put on a dark pair of sunglasses, not attempting to fix the black mascara smeared around my eyes.

On the bus to the airport, I thought about the job I had agreed on. I had so many reservations as everything wasn't explained to me in detail. I still didn't know what job I would be doing, but sometimes modeling jobs were like that. Okinawa was a familiar place, and I had some happy memories, so I couldn't imagine that anything could go wrong. The person that arranged the job for me, and the organizer of the party in Okinawa, was someone I knew fairly well, he helped me get other jobs before and he always acted in a professional manner. I tried to remind myself of that, but a creeping unease was unsettling me. I tried to recall the many conversations in the months prior and the organizer seemed genuinely excited about the concert. There wasn't any reason for me to feel this way. I dismissed it to nerves and tried to push the strange feelings aside.

I made it to the airport, hauling my two heavy luggage bags and one carry on behind me. I hadn't heard from Leo again, I imagined he would be boarding his flight for France, and then Italy, soon. There were a couple of reassuring phone calls from the party organizer, I will call him "T". He said that there would be a driver waiting for me at the exit when I landed in Okinawa, and a car would take me to my condo in Naha, where I would be spending the following 10 days. I never organized a party before. I didn't really know what the job would entail. "T" reassured me with a laugh, that it was going to be a piece of cake, I might have to run errands and there would be a car for me down in the garage.

Sitting on the airplane, I watched the sunset, as we passed over the Ryuku Island chain. The water was that same blue-green that I remembered, and a flood of memories came back of my family, my kids...my husband, and all of the hopes and dreams that were shattered in the years that followed. The last year in Okinawa, we both had tried, and it seemed like things would be okay, despite all the damage the separations had caused. Where did it all go wrong, and *how did I end up here*?

It was evening when we landed, and I quickly exited the airplane and claimed my bags. I spotted my driver right away, as there were hardly any people waiting at the exit. We greeted each other and he politely took my luggage, and told me the car was parked outside. A warm familiar breeze mingled with island flowers welcomed me, as we exited through the automatic doors, and I was led to a long white limousine that made me feel like a movie star.

That's when the reality of where I was hit me for the first time. I had never been so far from anyone that cared about me. I knew virtually no one in Okinawa, and if I got into any trouble I would be on my own. It was dark and raining when we finally arrived at the apartment that I would be using during my stay. It was not as fancy as I had hoped, a plain white building with four floors and external stairs. It reminded me of a cheap motel. The driver pointed to the elevator, said I was on the third floor, and asked if I needed help with my bags. I said no thank you, so he gave me the key to the apartment and departed.

I regretted overpacking as I hauled my luggage into the small elevator and ascended to the third floor. I found my door, and sweaty from the humid air, I put the key in and turned, but to my dismay, the door didn't open. *What the heck?* I pulled the key out and tried again, but still no luck, the key wasn't turning! There was a keypad with numbers and I slowly realized there must be a code. I stared at my key and shook my head. This was not starting out well. I tried "T," but I couldn't get a line. I looked around for the first time, and I could see lights down the road, there must be a payphone around, I would have to try to find one and call him again. There was no way I was going to carry my luggage with me, so I neatly placed it next to the wall beside my door, hoping I would find it there when I returned.

A Rainy humid night in Okinawa.

By the time I made it to the corner market and spotted a payphone, I was drenched. I tried "T" again, and to my relief I heard his familiar voice.

"Moshi, Moshi"

"Hey, it's Christy, I made it! I am in Okinawa at my apartment, but I

can't get in, Is there a code?"

"Of course there is, do you think I would make it easy for you?"

"I don't understand, it's raining and I am really tired, what's the code? I had to call you from a payphone, my mobile isn't working."

He laughed, but I didn't find anything humorous about any of it. He should have given me the code, what kind of game was he playing?

I asked him again for the code, and instead of giving it to me, he wanted to play a guessing game!

"What do you think the code is?"

I could feel that I was about to lose my temper. I took a deep breath and replied.

"If I knew what it was, do you think I would be standing at a payphone in the pouring rain, asking you for it?"

He must have heard the tension in my voice, because he gave in with a sigh, *"Your no fun, Chris...the code is your birthday."*

I said thanks and quickly hung up, and I spent the short walk back to the condo going over the conversation in my head. Maybe I was just over-tired and sensitive. *He was just joking, wasn't he?* It just felt like he was trying to control me! I read a lot of books in the past about foreign women that come to Japan to work and end up in a block of cement at the seaside. *But you know him, Christy.* He was a friend. We had several conversations in the month's prior, and there wasn't anything that wasn't professional about "T," I had no reason not to trust him, I was being paranoid.

Relieved to see that my bags were exactly where I left them when I arrived back to my apartment for the second time, I put the key in and punched in my birthday and this time the key turned. As the door opened with an angry groan, I was greeted by a musty smell. I entered into a small kitchenette with a sink, a hotplate, and small refrigerator. Pulling my luggage in behind me, I closed the door and walked down a narrow hallway to a second room. There was a bed, a chair, and a small television on a stand.

The bathroom was tiny, even for Japanese standards, I was so disappointed! I noticed a sliding glass door, the only way out in the entire place, aside from the front door, that opened to a small balcony with bars that were at least 6 feet high, that looked more like a cage. I took a step onto the balcony where I had a 360 view of my surroundings. I wasn't in an isolated place, there was a big parking garage next door, and plenty of restaurants and bars and shops scattered along the streets adjacent to the building.

I was startled out of my surveillance operation by the shrill ring of my cell phone, so I rushed inside and quickly fumbled for the tiny cell at the bottom of my handbag.

"Hello?"

"Hey, hey, hey, how's it going Chris? You make it in okay?"

"Yes." I tried to make my voice sound light and fun, but it was difficult.

"I will let you get settled in and come by later to say hello."

Wait...what does he mean, *later?* I looked at my watch, it was 9 pm already. I was tired, I just wanted to take a shower and go to sleep. I told him this, but he still insisted he would drop by to *just say hello* and explain some things about the job to me.

"Okay,"...I replied reluctantly, and hung up the phone.

I realized how thirsty I was so I went to the little refridgerator to see if there was anything in there to drink. There was an expensive bottle of champagne, but that was it. I should have bought something at that market on the corner, I would have to go back out and at least get some water. I sighed and quickly put my hair up in a ponytail and wiped the sweat off my face, then proceeded out of the door and down the block for the second time.

I returned 20 minutes later and filled the refridgerator with snacks and Japanese beer. I took a long drink of water and decided to freshen up. I didn't know when he would arrive, but it was a modeling job, after all, so I probably should look decent.

After about an hour of primping in the tiny bathroom, I decided to lay down, but as soon as my head hit the pillow I was fast asleep. A couple of hours passed before I was awakened by a knock. I stirred and glanced at my watch, Oh gosh, *it's almost midnight!* I rose quickly and padded to the front door in my barefeet. I opened the door, without asking who it was, and after 10 years I was face to face with a smiling "T."

"Wow, you look fantastic!"

I subconsciously smoothed out the wrinkles in the dress I had fallen asleep in.

"Sorry I fell asleep waiting, I am pretty tired."

He made his way in, looking the place over, as if he were seeing it for the first time. He admitted it wasn't great, but a friend was doing him a favor and it was all that was available in the summer months. I assured him it was fine. We stood in front of each other awkwardly, so I pulled up a chair to make a seating area and asked if he would like to sit down. He thanked me and sat on the bed instead, so I took the chair.

We made small talk, and then he explained a little of what my job duties would be in the next ten days. He said the most important thing is that I make the company look good, so I was to act in a professional manner, and if any of the other performers at the concert tried to flirt with me, I was to say I was with "T." He explained that sometimes backstage got wild, so I wasn't permitted to drink at all.

Because I don't like large crowds, I haven't attended many concerts in my life, so I could only use movies as a reference to imagine the wild parties that could go on backstage. The fact that when I drink too much I tend to black out, would keep my drinking in check. I didn't want to black out, I shuddered at the thought! Everything that he said up until that point helped me to relax quite a bit. I think he sensed that I wasn't as uptight, because he invited me out to a jazz bar around the corner for drinks. It was approaching 1 am, I guess this must be normal hours for him, so I reluctantly agreed.

We made our way down the street, the night air heavy with humidity. It was drizzling so we sprinted, and quickly ducked down a tiny alley until we reached a small inconspicuous red door and a flickering neon sign, that read *Jazz Times*. I could hear music coming from inside as I followed him through a beaded doorway to a small bar with tables scattered here and there. The place was empty. "T" said hello to his friend at the bar and then introduced me. I ordered a beer and we sat and made small talk.

He kept staring, which made me feel uncomfortable. I didn't want to send out any false signals, but the more nonchalant I acted, the more interested he became. He boasted of all of the women that come on to him because of his job, and that he was very selective on who he spent his time with.

Fantastic. I need to use the bathroom!

I politely excused myself. I could feel his eyes on me as I crossed the room. The uneasiness I felt from earlier in the evening was creeping back. Once in the safety of the bathroom, I gazed at myself in the mirror. I looked pale with shadows under my eyes, despite the makeup I used to try to cover them. My phone vibrated, and as I reached for it, I saw it was Leo! He told me that he had landed in France and would be boarding the plane for Italy shortly. I felt like I had been through so much and in all this time Leo was still flying! *Incredible.*

I reassured him everything was fine and that I missed him, *I felt so sad.* We didn't have plans to see each other again and his girlfriend in Rome would be picking him up at the airport. I needed to focus on this job in Okinawa. There wasn't any time to be sentimental. We said goodbye and he said that he would call later, but I reminded him of the time difference and to wait for my call instead. I didn't bother to tell him I was sitting at a bar with "T" drinking a beer. He was already jealous, and I didn't feel like answering a bunch of questions right then. I went back out to where I had left "T" sitting, and told him I was really tired, and asked if we could go back. He insisted on one more beer, so I reluctantly agreed.

I practically guzzled it and stood up, and to my relief he finally got the hint. As we exited the bar, the rain was really picking up, so much so, that by the time we reached the doorway of my apartment, we were both drenched. I wanted to bid him farewell and disappear inside, but he used the excuse that he wanted to dry off to come in. He followed me and disappeared into the small bathroom, using the *only* towel available to dry himself off, and then carelessly disgarded it on the floor. *Great.* I was hovering in the hallway, I didn't want to go into the bedroom area, I didn't want to give him the wrong idea. I announced that I was on the verge of collapse and that we should say our goodbyes.

"How are you going to survive the concert if you can't make it past 3 am," he joked. *"Did you see the bottle of champagne in the refridgerator?"*

"Yes, I did," I replied, stifling a yawn.
"Well what are you waiting for, let's open it! We have a lot to celebrate!" He moved past me into the kitchen, not waiting for my

protests.

I heard the cork pop, and moments later he returned with two champagne glasses filled to the rim.

"To old friendships," he said with a smile.

"Kampai!" I replied, and took a small sip. It was excellent champagne.

He moved a little closer to me. Now we were both standing in front of the bed. He took my glass from me and set it on the table, and told me to chill out and have a seat. There was a small CD player next to the television and for the first time I saw the collection of music next to it. It must be his, as it was out of place in the ambiance of the shoddy room. He put on a jazz cd and stared at me intently.

Oh god.

I stood up again.

"Okay, I don't want to give you the wrong idea, I am not interested in any kind of personal relationship with you. Maybe I should have made that clear earlier."

I guess it was a dropkick to his ego, because he became instantly annoyed.

"You knew what the deal was, don't try to back out now."

"What do you mean? I am interested in working for you at the concert, but that's it!" I exclaimed in a shaky voice, as my heart raced, attempting to fight back tears.

"We worked together before and there was never this kind of prerequisite," I tried to reason.

He could see how shaken up I was and he probably realized that I believed what I was saying, but it didn't stop him.

"*Stop being a little girl,*" he said as he sat on the bed, and then layed back on the pillow, making himself comfortable. He still had his shoes on, and a baseball hat!

"*I want you to leave, please. This is my room and you are invading my space now. I don't feel comfortable,*" tears that I couldn't hold back streamed down my face. He acted like he didn't hear me. He crossed his feet at the ankles and put his baseball cap over his face, letting out a long sigh.

"*You're overreacting Chris, come to bed,*" as he patted the place next to him.

I thought about leaving, but all of my things were scattered all over the room, and quite frankly, I had no energy left. This last altercation had taken everything out of me. I took the chair and moved it as far away from the bed as I could and then announced one last time that I wanted him to leave. He ignored me, so I curled up in the chair and I watched him from across the room with my most hateful stare.

I would sit there until morning and then I would leave, I decided. He was snoring loudly after 5 minutes, so I spent the rest of the night silently loathing him from my chair across the room. I wished him every possible bad luck imaginable as I drifted into a fitful sleep full of horrible nightmares.

The next morning I awakened to the sound of birds chirping as morning light slowly streamed in through the dirty balcony window. "T" stirred in his sleep and woke suddenly, as I quickly squeezed my eyes shut, doing my best to pretend I was asleep. He muttered to himself, and after 5 minutes he was up and moving about the room. I peered at him through half closed eyes as he took his wallet and keys off of the table and exited the apartment, not even looking back or saying anything to me.

Something told me to get up, so I did, and quickly followed his path to the door. I could hear a voice in my head exclaiming: *"DON'T LET THAT DOOR CLOSE, CHRISTY!"* It sounded like the voice of my father!

I put my hand on the door to keep it from closing. "T" was on the other side and was punching numbers in the keypad. I realized that he was probably changing the code, attempting to lock me in. I tried to be very still and control my breathing so he wouldn't hear me. After a couple of minutes, to my relief, I could hear him walking away. I don't know how long I stood there. I was afraid to move. Eventually, I stretched my reach to the kitchen counter and was able to prop the door with a cup from the kitchenette, making double sure, and then triple sure, that the door wasn't moving, because if it did, I was trapped!

I didn't have much time, I had to get out of there before he returned. I frantically called Leo, who answered in a cheerful voice, which quickly diminished when I explained to him what happened the night before. I had to listen to a lot of, *"I told you so's,"* as we had fought a couple of times about my so-called *"job"* in Okinawa. He told me to get out of there and call him when I was on my way to the airport. I didn't have time to take a shower, so I put on deodorant, brushed my teeth, ran a brush through my hair, slipped on my sandals, and wearing the same dress I slept in, I started gathering my belongings. I quickly packed up what was strewn about the room, making sure I had everything, and as a last thought, I grabbed my Japanese snacks from the refridgerator and stuffed them in my purse.

"T" took my key, along with his, so there wasn't any way for me to lock the door, I could only pull it shut. I tried to put my birthday into the number pad, but it didn't work anymore, he had changed the code, just as I suspected. I took off as fast as I could, down the elevator and out onto the street. I noticed a suspicious looking man on the other side of the road, and I don't know if I was just being paranoid, but when he saw me taking off down the road he quickly began talking on his cell phone.

Thank God my luggage had wheels, I thought, as I sprinted in the opposite direction as fast as I could go. The morning air was already hot and steamy and I began to sweat profusely. I didn't know where I was going, I just wanted to get as far away from the apartment as possible. I went up two streets, and then over two streets, in a criss cross pattern, when I eyed a taxi. I flagged it down, and threw my luggage on the backseat and got in, ignoring the polite protests from the taxi driver.

"I sorry, I do not go airport, you must take other taxi."

I panicked, *"Can you take me to another taxi?"*

The taxi driver agreed and took me to another taxi stand where taxis were waiting, ready to go to the airport. I paid the small fare and thanked him. The closer I got to the airport the more relieved I felt. I called Leo and reassured him I was okay and that I was on my way to the airport. He told me that he had called Benjamin Fulford and told him I was in trouble and warned me that he might be calling. I scolded him for doing that! I didn't like people knowing my business and Benjamin seemed like a person who would exaggerate.

I was able to buy a ticket to Tokyo, but I would have to spend most of the day at the airport, as the flight didn't leave until 8pm. I called my family in Colorado and let them know with a lot of excuses, that the job in Okinawa didn't work out, and I would be coming home early. Benjamin Fulford called me asking me what happened and if the *yakuza* was involved. He said he would go through his contacts and find out for sure, and let me know. I could sense the conspiracy theorist in him trying to come up with a conspiracy. There was no conspiracy! I stupidly trusted someone I shouldn't have trusted! I felt it was my fault and I still felt uneasy, even in the airport. I kept looking over my shoulder expecting to see "T" standing there.

The hours passed with a couple of more phone calls to Leo, before I finally boarded my plane with a heavy heart. Okinawa was my last chance, now I have nothing. I didn't make any money and in the end I had spent more than I should have. *What am I going to do?* I was too tired to think about it. As soon as I boarded the plane and settled in my seat, I was fast asleep, and then in what felt like just 5 minutes, we were landing at Haneda airport.

I decided that I would try to stay at the hotel by Narita airport again which is located on the other side of Tokyo. I had 9 days left before my flight back to America, I wasn't sure what I was going to do, but I needed a place to stay, at least for the night, and at least the hotel reminded me of Leo. I arrived at Haneda and as soon as I disembarked the plane, my cell phone rang. It was Benjamin Fulford, and in a manic rant he told me a bunch of stuff that he had found out about "T." Somehow he was linking what had just happened to me, to himself, and that the *yakuza* was sending *him* a message by doing this to me. It was complete bullshit, so I ignored him.

Benjamin asked me how I was going to get to Narita. I said I didn't know, maybe take a bus or the train. I thanked him, and told him I would call later when I was at the hotel, (something I had no intention of doing). He offered to come pick me up on his bike, but I had all of my luggage, so that would be pretty ridiculous, so I declined. I laughed to myself as I imagined riding on the back of Benjamin Fulford's rickety old bicycle, with my luggage stacked on top of my head.

Chapter 13

Tokyo again

I was short on cash, so I quickly found an ATM, but suddenly I couldn't remember my PIN and punched in the wrong number. I cancelled the transaction and started again, this time getting it right. I carefully removed my card and money, placing it carefully in my billfold, but as I walked away from the ATM, I was chased down by a little Japanese man.

"Simasen, Simasen!" (*Excuse me!*)

I quickly turned around as a Japanese man came running towards me waving my billfold! I had forgotten it next to the ATM!

I bowed deeply, *"Arigato gozaimasu!!!"* I was so thankful! He was pretty pleased with himself, flashing a huge smile as he watched me take off towards the shuttle. Only in Japan would someone chase you down to return your wallet. What good people. Angels were definitely watching over me on this trip, but how many more mistakes can I make? I needed to get my act together as I gave myself a verbal bashing that was audible to everyone around me. I didn't care anymore. I felt half mad!

Apparently both trains and buses stopped running at 11 pm, and it was well past that now. Realization slowly dawned on me that I was stuck on the other side of Tokyo. I had two choices, I could sleep at the airport and wait until morning to take a shuttle, or I could suck it up and take a taxi to the hotel. The driver and I joked that it was probably the most expensive taxi ride ever, as I arranged the yen carefully in his outstretched hand. Benjamin called me then, and asked if I was at the hotel. I said yes, and he told me he had called ahead and arranged a room for me. He was acting like it was a big deal, so I thanked him three times. He had just made a reservation, but he was acting like he had paid for the room!

By the time I made it to my room, all I could do was collapse on the bed. My cell phone rang. It was Leo. I told him I was safe at my hotel and I would figure the rest out as I went. Benjamin called again, trying to make plans with me for sightseeing the next day, but I really just wanted to get the heck out of Japan at that point. What could be worse than what I had been through already? Nine days stuck with Benjamin Fulford, that's what!

I paced in front of the window that looked out onto the parking lot far below. I was higher up this time, but it didn't make me feel any safer. I was worried that someone had followed me, or that the yakuza were watching me. "T" knew what hotel I was staying at before, because he had sent my ticket to Okinawa to it. He could show up here! That settled it. I couldn't stay here another day, I had to leave!

I looked up the number and called Nippon airlines, and luckily, I was able to change my ticket for the next evening. I could leave in the morning and spend the day at the airport until my flight departed.

I woke up the next morning, got dressed as fast as I could, and boarded the shuttle to the airport. It's really amazing what you can do, and how fast you can do it, when you have to. I spent a leisurely day strolling around the airport, buying gifts for everyone and dodging calls from Benjamin. I talked to Leo off and on the whole day, and recapped every detail of my misadventures to him. We both agreed, I was pretty lucky. When

I hung up with Leo my phone immediately rang. It was "T"! *Oh my God*! Okay, I think it's time to dispose of this disposable phone. I called Leo and told him I would contact him again when I got to L.A., that "T" was calling me, I had to get rid of my phone.

I carefully placed it in the envelope provided when I ordered the phone from America, and dumped it in the required bin on my way through security. *Goodbye Japan.* I hope I can come back again some day under better circumstances. Little did I know, it would be my last trip. I am always sad to think about that. Fukushima is going to change the face of the planet, not just Japan. I read recently that the train that Leo and I took from Narita airport to the center of Tokyo has extremely high levels of radiation. When people who rode the train were asked if they were aware of the danger, they just shrugged it off, ignoring the question.

I eventually made it back to America, my crazy adventure was finally over. I hadn't made the money that I had anticipated making, but I learned a valuable lesson, if something sounds too good to be true, it probably is! I got a nasty email from "T" threatening me a few days later. I decided that I didn't want anything from him, so I sent him back the money his company had spent on the plane ticket. I told him to never contact me again, and blocked his email. I heard later from friends in Japan, that his whole company went bankrupt after the earthquake and tsunami in 2011.

Chapter 14

Decisions, Decisions

My return to America was bittersweet, I was happy to be back with my kids again, but I missed Leo terribly. We tried to talk on the phone, but it wasn't the same. After spending so much time together, it was even harder to be apart, and not surprisingly, the problems in my marriage were worse than before. I daydreamed a lot, remembering every moment I spent with Leo and how special it was. I wasn't the only one having problems with our separation, Leo broke up with his girlfriend in Rome shortly after his return from Japan, and once he did that, he wanted a commitment from me.

Packing up for a week was different than living with a person and packing up your life. It felt impossible to me! I looked at all of the things I had accumulated throughout the years, the photo albums, knick-knacks, and momento's. There were so many memories. My oldest son was preparing to join the military and had just graduated from high school. My youngest son supported me, wanted me to make a change, but that would mean leaving him with his father. I just couldn't imagine doing that. Since I returned home my husband was drinking less, but we still had all of the problems we always had. It was a very difficult time for me and I suffered from depression. I was afraid to stay where I was, but I was afraid to move forward.

Two months passed and I was slowly dying inside. Leo was

so far away and the phone calls weren't making it any easier. I decided to make another trip back to Rome in August, and strategically timed it for when my kids would be with their grandparents for summer vacation. I would have been sitting at home miserable, so I planned a trip for 2 weeks. It would be the longest time we would spend together.

Leo found an apartment in a small medieval village in the mountains, 45 minutes from Rome, close to where his mother lived. It even had a castle, it sounded perfect! It was a new place and we could make our own memories there. I think at that point I still hoped something would happen between us that would change my mind about our relationship, so I could return quietly to my miserable life and tough it out as I always had. On the flight to Rome for the second time that year, thoughts about how unstable my life felt ran through my mind. I had made a lot of excuses to my husband, and he reluctantly let me take the trip, but I think that he knew deep down that it was over between us. I had been so distant, if he didn't notice just how distant I was, we had no right to be together.

Leo voiced his opinion every day on how much he wanted me there with him in Italy. I tried to enjoy being together, but we were on a timer again, and each passing day was one day less that we had together. I can write paragraph upon paragraph on how hard it was and how much I cried. Divorce is never easy, and usually there are these kinds of feelings...especially when only one person wishes to leave the marriage. I still talked to my husband, and at one point my phone accidentally dialed him and he heard Leo in the background! This was getting ugly. I think that was when I decided once and for all to leave, but more importantly, *to take action.*

Enjoying every moment together. August 2009.

I said goodbye to Leo for the third time and boarded the plane for America. I loved Leo with all of my heart. I could *feel* the force of the universe pushing us together, and I couldn't fight it any longer! When I returned home, I had many long talks with my children and I tried to talk to my husband, but it was just a repeat of when I tried to leave him before. There were a lot of promises to change, but I knew from past experience they were empty promises.

I spent many tearful afternoons going through all of my wordly possessions and packed up what I could into three boxes that I shipped to Italy. I couldn't take my youngest son with me, that was the part that killed me the most. An American can't go live in Italy just because they want to, I was on a tourist visa and wouldn't be able to stay more than three months. I was going to apply for residency, but that proved to be much more difficult than I had ever imagined, and even more impossible for my son. He reassured me he would be fine and so we planned for him to visit me when he wasn't in school and when I looked in his eyes I understood that he would keep his promise.

I went back and forth from Italy to America two more times, where I received very little support from my side of the family. My sister didn't say much, but my brother let me know what he thought about me leaving. I think he was angry that I was leaving the country more than a marriage I was unhappy in. My brother never got along with my husband and there was always a lot of animosity between the two, so I couldn't understand why he was so against me leaving him. Was happiness so much to ask for? I was tired of all of the people around me voicing their opinions and attacking me for doing what they didn't have the courage to do! In the end, you can't listen to other people's opinions.

Initially leaving my marriage was the most difficult thing that I have ever had to do, but I am happy I had the courage to do it. Marriage vows are sacred and should last a lifetime, but life is sacred too...*and we all deserve to be happy!*

Nick's graduation from high school, May 2009.

Chapter 15

The story of Rambo

Arcylic on paper 2015, by the me

I t was autumn of 2008 when I received an unexpected call from a friend who said that there was a chihuahua that was up for adoption at the pet hospital in town. She thought it was ironic, because just the week before during a lunch conversation I expressed how much I wanted a chihuahua. I was really lonely and I thought it would be nice to have a little dog to love. The circumstances surrounding how Rambo came into my life were pretty miraculous, so I thought I would briefly share them with you.

A few days prior, there had been an accident in the canyon, that involved a minivan with a family of 5 on board, and a semi-truck, and everyone in town was sad about it. It had happened at 5 am, when going around a curve, a minivan collided with a semi-truck, tragically killing the whole family. There was a hard case pet carrier found in the field next to accident, but no animal, so it was assumed that the family pet had also perished in the accident. Two days later, a small dog was found wandering around one of the ranches located close to where the accident occurred. He was found crouched down in a barn by the family dog. That's when the police were called, and also my friend who lived in a ranch next to the accident.

The surroundings are wild, with many predators that live in the area. Rambo had scratches all over his body and his ear was ripped, so he obviously had to defend himself against the creatures of the wild. There were coyotes, wolves, mountain lions, bears, moose, elk, and so many other animals that could have harmed him, yet he managed to survive. He was the talk of the town! I raced down to the pet hospital and that was when I saw Rambo for the first time shivering in his cage. I held him in my arms and tried to soothe him, but he continued to shake. I wanted to take him home right then, but I would have to wait 5 days, in case someone from the extended family wanted to claim him, but thankfully the 5 days passed and I was able to adopt him and bring him home.

Aside from my recent trips abroad, we were inseparable. He slept with me and I took him everywhere I went. I didn't have any babies to hold and he was perfect to cuddle and love. There didn't seem to be enough time to gather all of the paperwork that I needed to take him on an international flight, but with the help of my mother's husband, I was able to get all of the vaccinations and paperwork I needed in just one day. Despite all of the hard feelings in the past about my mother's divorce, and what happened to my father...I think I was able to forgive him with this act of kindness. I felt like I didn't have anyone on my side and having the support of my mother and stepfather really helped.

Rambo moves to Italy.

Feeling carefree in Rome.

Happy together.

Chapter 16

Life in Italy

I have lived in foreign countries before, Germany when my family was stationed there from 1980-1983, and Okinawa, as I mentioned earlier. But they were military bases, and it is completely different than living in a foreign country as an expat. We wanted to make sure that I followed all of the rules, so within 8 days of arriving, I visited the immigration office (*questura*), and filled out all of the paperwork. I was receiving $500 every two weeks of support from my husband, and that would be proof enough that I could sustain myself.

Leo's mother accompanied me on many trips to the immigration office, which was definitely an experience that we both still talk about. I always felt privileged to be an American, but when you are standing in line with all of the others, everyone is the same. I admit that I flashed my American passport around. I wanted everyone to know I was American!

I was photographed and fingerprinted and told that my "*permesso di soggiorno*" or residency permit was in process and that it could take up to three months to receive an answer. In the meantime, I had a receipt that I could show if stopped by the *carabinieri* (local police), that demonstrated that I was waiting for my permit.

I didn't know at the time, but the Italian judicial system is a joke, and most everything that has to go through any type of legal process takes much longer than anywhere else.

I initially liked living in the small village in the "Valley of Tears," a beautiful valley with monasteries and ancient ruins close by. I focused on the fact that Leo and I were together now, and soon my son would be coming to visit. It was always important to me that my children be introduced to different cultures. It was one of the reasons I chose Okinawa in 1997. I had traveled to Italy before on vacation, but as a tourist you never experience a place like you do when you live there.

Exploring the castle in Roviano.

Funny little family.

Getting to know each other.

Me and Leo.

Our little two story apartment was cozy and perfect for us. With the money that Leo received from publishing books in Japan with Benjamin Fulford we were able to buy all of the things we needed to make our home together. I fixed up my son's room and took pictures to show him. I wanted him to know that he had a special place in Italy. I wasn't in contact with my oldest son because he was at Marine Corps boot camp, but I thought about him every day. Since we couldn't talk, I tried to send him psychic messages, hoping he could hear me. Many nights I woke up in a cold sweat after dreaming about the horrible drills he must be experiencing.

Chapter 17

Benjamin Fulford comes to visit

L eo kept in touch with Benjamin Fulford during the months that followed our trip to Tokyo. One morning, Leo received a message that he would be coming to Italy and wanted to meet with some of Leo's contacts. There were some Japanese citizens that Benjamin knew who had been traveling with gold bonds which had been confiscated by the Italian police. Benjamin Fulford hoped that Leo, with his vast array of contacts, could help release the bonds from police custody. Leo goes into detail about it in Volume 2 of his *Confessions*, so I will just explore my perspective on what happened.

Leo with Benjamin Fulford in Rome.

We have an apartment in Rome that the family shares, and Leo offered to guest Benjamin for a couple of days. We greeted him at the entrance of the flat and I was astonished at how much Benjamin had deteriorated in just a few months! He was now walking with a cane, wheezing, and snorting as he tried to navigate the five flights of stairs

We drove into Rome one evening to have dinner with Benjamin at the same restaurant that we shared our first meal together. It had become our favorite place, and everyone that came through Rome to visit us was taken there. Leo invited an old friend who was a fan of Benjamin Fulford's blog, so there were four of us at dinner. I sat across from Benjamin, and because Leo was so busy catching up with his old friend, I was stuck in awkward conversation. Would you believe that he continued to insist that what happened to me in Okinawa was a message to him from his enemies?

I stared at him incredulously.

"You don't say?" I humored, as I (*again*) realized he suffered from a super-inflated ego. The conversation took a bizarre turn, when out of the blue Benjamin began explaining vaginal secretions to me, *in detail!* I cleared my throat and kicked Leo under the table, totally losing my appetite for the lobster linguine placed in front of me.

Leo was listening to everything that was being said on the sly, and we had a laugh about it afterward. Benjamin was still coughing, snorting, and wheezing. We imagined he must be on drugs, or coming off of drugs. He wasn't acting normal, or even like a person who had caught a cold on the plane coming over.

Day two of Benjamin's trip to Rome. He would be traveling by train to Milan to meet a couple of Leo's business associates that might be able to help with the bonds. In the end, Benjamin was told that there wasn't anything that could be done, the bonds weren't even legal, and none of Leo's contacts wanted to deal with them.

I don't know if this is what motivated Benjamin Fulford to attack Leo, something that would last up until this very day! He went back home to Japan, and a short while later the attacks from his blog began. He accused Leo of trying to have him murdered in Milan, that he was given poison that obstructed his breathing, and even crazier accusations!

He called Leo a Satanist, which I found pretty ironic, remembering a conversation after dinner, when Benjamin tried over and over to convince Leo to conjure a demon as if it were a party trick! Leo denounced the occult a long time ago and he stressed this to Fulford. To me, it seemed like Benjamin Fulford was the Satanist and when he didn't find the companion in evil that he had hoped to find in Leo, *he turned on him.*

In this age of deception, he is just another disinfo agent and I hope more people will open their eyes to the false propaganda that he is spewing. Leo was able to defend himself by writing and documenting his experience with Benjamin Fulford and those screwy bonds in his book, *Confessions, Vol 2.* It's a fascinating story, better told by Leo, so check it out!

Chapter 18

Farewell Elio Zagami

One rainy morning at the beginning of March, we were awakened by a frantic phone call from Leo's mother.

"Papa è morto!"

We scrambled out of bed, and I think we flew the 15 minutes that it took to reach Leo's mother. We drove so fast the tires of the car barely touched the ground, but we arrived to a grim scene. Leo's father woke up that morning like any other morning, showered, shaved, and dressed. As he sat on the edge of the bed, putting on his socks and shoes, he suffered a fatal heart attack. Leo's mother found him on the floor in the bedroom on his back, with only one sock on. As we arrived, the ambulance and doctors were leaving. He had been announced dead 15 minutes before.

Remembering my reaction when my father died, I found Leo's mother to be very composed during the most difficult time in her life, when I seemed to be the complete opposite when I was faced with death.

Leo and Elio one month before he passed.

We spent the following days in a fog. To add to the gloom, it rained incessantly for a week. It seemed the sun would never shine again. The funeral arrangements were made quickly, and friends and family came to view Elio, who was placed in the living room. The only funeral that I attended was my father's, and since he was cremated, I wasn't able to see him again to say goodbye. It amazed me how alive Elio looked. It seemed he would crack into one of his wonderful smiles that would light up the room at any moment. It made me very sad. I stood over him and sighed deeply. We had just seen each other a couple of days before for lunch and now he was gone. I remembered sitting next to him on Sunday, while he smiled and poured me wine. He was different than everyone, much like Leo, and I felt so sad that I would never know him more. I wished I had spent more time with him, asked him more questions, listened more. I guess those are the regrets we all have when we lose someone we love.

Leo and his father.

Leo's father died on March 10, and Tony was set to arrive on the 21st. I remembered the days and weeks after my own father's death and how I could barely function, which led me to admire the Zagami's. They pushed their own sadness aside to greet Tony with loving, open arms.

Tony was really happy to see me again and to be in Italy. We spent 8 days together that went by too fast, exploring Rome and the area around where we live. I think it helped to take Leo's mind away from his sadness.

Before I knew it my son was boarding the return flight to America. I was constantly choking back tears lately. How can one be so happy and so sad, at the same time? Watching my son walk away from me, knowing it would be months until I would see him again, caused unrelenting sorrow, even when I think about it now. *"Stiff upper lip, darling!"* I took a deep breath. I needed to be strong. But there was something else that was weighing heavy on my mind... *I was pregnant.*

Tony in Roviano.

Putting on a brave smile.

Chapter 19

More loss, more sadness

When I told Leo I was pregnant he was elated. His bitter divorce had left him without contact with his son, something that hurt him deeply, and a baby would heal a lot of that hurt. Being a mother has been my greatest joy in life, so to find myself pregnant at 38 years old was such a blessing.

Talking about the baby helped to ease some of the pain of losing Elio. I was only 5 weeks pregnant, and decided I would go to see a doctor in another week. Luckily, I was able to acquire a medical card, even though I didn't have my residency yet. It allowed me to use the Italian healthcare system for free, and I was relieved for that. It was one less thing I had to worry about. Leo wanted me to see a private doctor, and had a friend who suggested a wonderful female doctor that spoke perfect English in Rome. The appointment was made for the beginning of June, which was the first slot she had open. I wished I could have gone earlier, but it was important to me that I had a female doctor that spoke English, so I patiently waited.

April turned to May, as the summer slowly approached. A couple of days before my 39th birthday I felt mild cramps and saw blood. I reached back in my memory to when I was pregnant before, and with both my previous pregnancies the same thing had happened. I also spoke to Leo's mother, and she agreed it could be normal. I was supposed to see the doctor in a couple of days anyway, so I took it easy and tried to rest.

The cramps persisted. I spent countless hours googling if cramps were normal during the first trimester and I barely slept that night. To my horror, I realized that the cramps I was experiencing were coming like timed contractions! The next morning, I called Leo's mother and told her that I think I should go to the emergency room, that I was still bleeding and the cramps hadn't let up. She agreed and decided we all go together in Leo's car. We arrived at an ancient hospital in Subiaco, and the OB/GYN ward was nothing short of medieval.

Jessica announced that it was an emergency, that I was pregnant, and a wheelchair magically appeared. I was taken to one room, and than to another and I was asked a lot of questions in Italian that Jessica translated for me. The ultrasound confirmed that I had had a miscarriage, but I would have to have an operation. I was heartbroken. Leo and I held each other and cried. A couple of nuns came in and looked at us with sympathy. I would have to be admitted for the afternoon, but at least I could leave in the evening.

I was prepped for surgery and rolled down the hall to an elevator. I felt like I was descending into a dungeon, and Leo wasn't permitted to accompany me, so I felt alone and scared. I was wheeled into an operating room that looked more like an ancient torture chamber. I glanced over at the row of surgical tools on the cold steel table and I shivered. A women appeared, and asked me a few questions in English, then gave me an anesthetic. The thin paper that covered my naked body kept slipping, and even in my drugged state, I tried to cover myself. Just as I was drifting off, I thought I saw two men appear, who looked more like construction workers than medical staff. I tried to cover myself again, as I felt myself drifting off, with the thought that they were looking at my naked body as I lay there unconscious.

Chapter 20

Happy Birthday to me

I spent my first birthday in Italy recovering from my miscarriage and I forced myself to be brave. My son would be arriving for the summer and I wanted to have the best time with him, so we planned wonderful trips together. First we would go to Sicily and later we would take a trip to Monte Carlo for a British family reunion that had been much anticipated. I was excited to show Tony exciting new places, so I switched my focus from mourning everything I had lost, to celebrating all the wonderful things in my life.

We took a train, and than a boat, to the small island of Alicudi, located off the coast of Italy, in the Aeolian island chain, where Leo's Sicilian grandfather came from. It was rustic, peaceful, and romantic. It seemed the sea and the island breeze healed me, because I felt much better when we were there. We ate wonderful seafood, spent days exploring the island, and laying on the beach. What made me the happiest was seeing how well my son was adjusting to everyone, and to life in Italy. I hugged him close to me, but I missed my oldest son… I had invited him to come to Italy whenever he wanted, but he was going through a lot of changes himself, including adjusting to military life.

My first birthday in Italy, the day after my miscarriage...smiling through tears.

Tony enjoying the beach with Jessica.

Leo and his mom.

Leo and Christy in Alicudi.

I am healed by the sea.

After a couple of weeks on an island in the middle of nowhere, we returned to Rome, and then to the mountains. We had an action packed summer planned, we were going to Monte Carlo next! We decided to drive there and meet Leo's extended family in a hotel that was booked especially for the family gathering. We would drive to Lucca, a small city about half way, and spend the night, before proceeding on to France. Little did I know that we would never make it there.

The tranquil beauty of Alicudi.

Chapter 21

My arrest!

In planning the excursion to Monte Carlo, I religiously visited the immigration office every week to check on my status. I was always greeted with the same answer, it was still in process. I was also given a website I could visit to see when my permit updated, so I wouldn't have to stand in line to find out the same answer.

We piled into a rental car and took off on our adventure one bright, sunny morning in early July. We drove the scenic highway that took us through Umbria, arriving in Tuscany, where we had lunch. We leisurely made it to Lucca, stopping and taking pictures along the way. I usually book hotels ahead of time, but we decided to stop at a random one along the highway. We had a nice afternoon and evening and enjoyed the food and music of the region very much. Since we had to wake up the next morning to continue our journey to France, we turned in early.

The next morning we woke, and Leo and my son went down to the breakfast room, while I showered. I was still in the shower when I heard the hotel phone ring, and I let Leo know when he returned with my croissant and coffee. I was just drying off when the phone rang again, and Leo promptly answered it. I heard an exchange in Italian, and then Leo appeared in the bathroom and told me that they needed to see me down in the lobby immediately, there was a problem with my passport. I have never been in trouble before, not even a traffic ticket, I tried to imagine what it could be. I had just checked the website for my permesso status, and it was the same as always...*In Process*.

I quickly pulled on a skirt and top, and slipped on my flipflops, as I grabbed my purse on the way out of the door. My hair was sopping wet, so I quickly twisted it in a knot, and pinned it up. On the way down in the elevator, I tried to reassure myself that everything was fine, I had followed all of the rules. I had my little receipt to show that I was going through the *permesso* procedure. As the elevator doors opened, I was greeted by two stern looking *polizia* officers.

That's when my heart began to race. *Was I in trouble?* They didn't speak English, but quickly explained to Leo in rapid Italian that I must accompany them to the *questura*, that there was a problem with my passport, and they would let me know when I got there. They wouldn't tell me anything else! I almost started crying, but I held back my tears. I was in the middle of a busy lobby, and all of the tourists were staring at me like I was a criminal!

They agreed to let me drive with Leo and Tony (and Rambo) to the police station just outside the walls of the little city. I cried on the way, and Leo reassured me that everything would be fine, but he cursed at how absurd it was. I should have called the American embassy right then and there, but everything was happening so fast, I didn't even think about it.

They wouldn't let Tony and Rambo come in, so they had to wait for me anxiously in the rental car in the hot July sun. On entering the *questura*, I was reminded of a documentary I had watched recently about an American college student named Amanda Knox, who was arrested in Italy for murder, and in the end spent many years in an Italian prison not far from where I was now, before she was acquitted and able to return to America. Leo was outraged that I was being treated in this way, especially when there were illegal immigrants from Africa taking over Italy, and he voiced his opinion to the officer.

It was explained to me that my *"permesso"* was denied, and there was no explanation as to why. I would have to leave the country within 2 weeks, or obtain a lawyer and appeal the decision for deportation. Of course, I would have to do the latter, which ended up costing 2,500 euro, and in the end it didn't even get me my permesso! The officer agreed that it was outrageous, and explained I would be able to stay in Italy while my case was in appeal. We explained that we were on our way to France, but he advised that I shouldn't leave Italy.

I was so relieved that I wasn't being arrested, that I didn't care about the trip to Monte Carlo. Tony was visibly shaken, and so relieved to see me. I apologized to him for having to wait in the car, and promised that we would do something special on the way back to Rome. We returned to the hotel, and gathered our belongings, leaving Lucca behind. We stopped in Pisa on the way back to Rome, and the rest of the month was spent wrapped up in Italian bureaucracy. We found a lawyer to defend my case, but we had to come up with 2,500 euro. Money was tight, so I decided to sell some things on ebay to come up with the cash, which amazingly I was able to do!

Trying to forget the trauma of that morning, Leo and Christy leaving Lucca.

In the end, I became so frightened of traveling that we were careful of every place we stayed, and I definitely couldn't leave Italy. Anytime I went anywhere, I was required to carry a folder around with me with my court case, to prove that my status was in appeal. I was never notified that my *permesso* was declined, and that was something that really angered me. I realized that in this country you could do everything right, and still find yourself in trouble. Lucca is known to be a Masonic town and Leo had a few enemies there. He wondered if maybe someone had alerted the police, to shake him up. It's all speculation, and in the end it could just be Italian incompetence.

I made the best of the rest of the summer with Tony. We spent time traveling around Rome, but we didn't vacation outside of the region. Another heartfelt goodbye at the airport ended my summer, tainted by the terrible experience we had shared.

Heartbroken every time I had to say goodbye.

In the short time that I had been in Italy, my *dolce vita* perspective of the country had shattered. I was living through rose colored glasses before, and once the shades were off, I began to notice how dirty Rome was, how many beggars there were, how many illegal immigrants walked around doing whatever they wanted, and how many people were living in poverty because of the crisis.

It was also a tough time in my relationship with Leo. I really wanted to go back home to America, but if I left Italy, I wouldn't be able to return. I felt like a prisoner! My son graduated from Marine Corps bootcamp and I was unable to attend. It was an important event in my son's life and I was stuck in Italy. I didn't make any friends and the villagers in Roviano didn't welcome me. When I walked to the park to take my dog for a walk everyday, I noticed the whispers much more than I had before. I tried to be friendly, but most of the time I was shunned. I missed my family, I missed my children, I wasn't adjusting well.

There were many heated arguments that would end with me packing up all of my belongings in a crying fit, only to have to unpack it all. I loved Leo so much, but I hated him for taking me so far away from everyone I loved. I needed someone to blame, and he was the only one I could take my frustrations out on. He confessed his love for me, at times on his knees begging me not to leave him. *No one has ever loved me so much.*

Nick graduating from Marine Corps boot camp, San Diego, California.

Realistically, I knew that I couldn't live without him, and if I left, I would regret it.

We finally experienced a bit of good luck when Leo was approached by an Italian publisher who wanted to publish the *Confessions* that he blogged about since 2006, when he came out of the Monte Carlo P2 Masonic Lodge. He was one of the first to expose the dark side of the Illuminati from the inside, with documentation and real life experiences. Leo happily agreed and signed a contract. Leo made a lot of prophetic realizations in his interviews, and he had many that followed his work in Italy, and abroad. It was the fall of 2010, and Leo began writing his *Confessions* that would be later published in English.

Leo finding inspiration in his father's studio.

Chapter 22

Estonia

L eo hosted a radio program in his early teens, and when he was older he became a successful DJ in Italy and then in London, after moving there in the early 90s. He produced a lot of music during that time and traveled all over the world to a variety of exotic places including Iceland, Scandinavia, Russia, and Berlin. During that time, Leo was initiated into the Masonic world and did a lot of investigative work in tandem to his Dj career. For some, it may seem strange that Leo would be able to juggle such different careers, but if you listen to the music that Leo produced with titles such as Cosmic Land and The Magickal Child, you could easily understand that Leo's music is drenched in esoteric knowledge with the use of *special frequencies.*

In November 2010, we were invited to Tallinn, Estonia by one of Leo's old friends who was organizing a cultural event and wanted Leo to play give an interview to Estonian National Radio. Leo had been to Estonia many times, but it was a new place for me. My Italian lawyer told me I could travel within the EU without having to show my passport, but I felt uneasy traveling with my experience in Lucca in the back of my mind. We arrived mid-day and was greeted by Leo's DJ friend who gave us a ride to our hotel. Leo would be playing from 1- 3am that night.

Tallinn, Estonia November 2010.

Christy and Leo exploring Tallinn.

Beautiful architecture.

exploring the town.

Kumu art museum- Soviet and Estonian artwork.

We had plenty of time to explore the town, so we bundled up and headed out. It was only November, but to me it felt brutally cold. I had just moved from Colorado to Italy, so I understood what freezing temperatures felt like, but nothing prepared me for the ice cold flurry that assaulted us as we made our way to the local cake shop for an evening *aperitive.*

As we stumbled into the café, we bumped into an old man on his way out. Leo quickly apologized, but when hearing Leo's accented English, the man's demeanor quickly changed. He replied in Estonian, and Leo again apologized, saying he didn't speak Estonian, the man sneered, *"Of course you don't."* We stood in a triangle, and what probably amounted to only a couple of minutes, felt like hours. The man stared at me with his black eyes and I felt a cloud of darkness descend upon us. He suddenly put his left hand inside his overcoat, as if he were fondling something underneath. I quickly grabbed Leo by the arm, pulling him into the warm safety of the cake shop.

We stood silently as we waited for our turn to order. As we made our way to a table in the corner of the room, it felt like everyone was staring at us with the same black eyes as the old man. We sat in silence as I sipped my tea with shakey hands.

Leo after the encounter with the black magician.

"What the heck was wrong with that guy?" I finally blurted out. We were usually so talkative, the silence between us felt deafening.

"We have to be careful. Leo replied. *"That guy was a shaman. There are some powerful dark magicians in Estonia, and I have a lot of enemies."*

He explained to me that Estonia had escaped Russian domination many times and that there is a prominent dislike for Russians by the local people as the last units of the Russian army left in August 1994. There is also a strong presence of black magic that was practiced heavily in the region by magicians since ancient times.

"*I could feel the dark energy,* I replied, *I think he had something in his coat.*"

I never experienced a psychic attack before, let alone an attack that was so evil in nature. I was shaken up and scared. I said the Our Father prayer silently to myself as I finished my tea, and we exited into the dark, cold night. I jumped at shadows on the way back to the hotel, I couldn't escape the uneasy feeling I had.

We didn't say much for the rest of the evening, Leo silently worked on his computer, as I dressed for dinner. That evening we would be dining with Leo's friend and his wife, who picked us up around 8pm. The dinner was pleasant and we were able to put the negative experience behind us for a few hours.

Leo at dinner, having, you guessed it! Borsch!

Outside walls of the town.

Medieval architecture, with McDonalds in the background.

The theater holding the cultural event was conveniently located adjacent to the hotel, and on the way home we decided to go there and check out the equipment and DJ booth. It was around 11 pm and a line of people were already wrapped around the side of the building waiting to get in. I couldn't understand how they could bear to stand outside in the cold and wait, but it was encouraging to see that so many had shown up.

As Leo made his way to the DJ booth, I sat in one of the seats in the front row, observing the scene around me. As I scanned the room, I noticed an older man in the distance, standing in the aisle, staring at me, I instinctively looked away, but when I looked back he was gone. I stood up quickly, *we have to get out of here!* I spotted Leo talking to one of the technicians, so I quickly gathered up my belongings and hurried to his side.

"Are you ready?" I asked. When Leo glanced over at me, he saw I was anxious to go, so he announced that he would see everyone in a couple of hours and we quickly headed for the exit. I decided not to mention the incident to Leo. We were both on edge, and I didn't want to make matters worse. I knew that Leo needed to concentrate on playing that evening, and I didn't want to disturb him with what I think I might have seen and how I was feeling, which wasn't very good.

Back at the hotel I tried to relax, but all I could do was pace the room. Through the window, I watched the theater from above, trying to spot if someone that might look like the person I saw earlier was lurking below. The tiny people all looked the same, bundled in their coats, hunched against the cold. I looked over at Leo, who must have been concentrating on something very interesting on his computer, because he didn't look up at me at all as I paced back and forth in front of him. I decided to take a bath and start getting ready. I would be assisting that night, and I wanted to try and snap out of the doom and gloom mood I was in.

I tried to relax in the bath, but every time I closed my eyes, I saw the black eyes of the magician staring back at me. I attempted to put a light of protection around me, something that I had done dozens of times before in meditation, but when I tried over and over again to picture white light above me, something that was so easy to do in the past, became nearly impossible.

I quickly dressed and began applying my makeup. As I stood before the mirror I noticed that the face that stared back at me appeared to be far, far away. I felt like I was looking at myself from another perspective! Thoughts that didn't feel like my own came into my mind.

I was doing all of this for Leo, and all he could do was ignore me. How can he ignore me? How can he treat me like this?

What happened next is something that I have spent many sleepless nights thinking about.

I exited the bathroom to find Leo in the same position I had left him earlier. I was angry and let him know it. He responded quickly in anger, as we threw insults at each other.

"I'm not going to your stupid gig, you can carry your other bag of records yourself!" I screamed, not caring who heard me.

Leo rose off the bed and came at me, and to my horror his eyes had turned that same black as the man in the theater! He grabbed me by my arms and shook me hard, throwing me across the room. I hit the wall like a rag doll and fell to the floor, twisting my knee. He quickly picked me up off the ground and threw me on the bed, jumping on top of me. I fought as hard as I could, using my legs to defend myself as I tried to push him off of me. I kicked him in his hand and it was enough for him to retreat as he grabbed his fingers, stating I broke one of them.

Everything felt surreal, but this feeling quickly went away when I was faced with the chaos of what had just happened.

"I am sorry, I didn't mean it! You just threw me across the room! Look at my knee!" I cried, pointing at the bloody bruise that was forming.

When Leo saw my blood he screamed, *"Noooo, this isn't happening!"* and collapsed backward on the bed. I stood over him in shock as he thrashed back and forth, with his eyes rolled back, foam escaping his mouth. I ran to the bathroom and retrieved a glass of water, attempting to give it to him, but he thrashed away from me in another convulsion, muttering something I couldn't understand.

"What are you saying, I don't understand!"

He was speaking in a language that wasn't Italian, his hurt hand raised above his head. His body seemed to rise up off of the bed, so I instinctively jumped on him, pushing him back down...For the second time since arriving to Estonia, I was reciting the Our Father from my Catholic childhood. I covered his face with kisses and kept repeating *I love you , I am sorry, I love you, I am sorry*...over and over again. Tears streamed down my face as I kissed his tears away. Suddenly he began to cough and sputter.

"*Water,*" he gasped. I jumped up and grabbed the bottle of water and he drank it in one gulp, wanting more. He downed a second bottle as I told him to take deep breaths and try to relax. He seemed to be recovering when he jumped up spontaneously, yelling, "*This can't happen to me, I am too powerful for this to happen!*"

I looked at his hand, and asked him to move it. It was hurt, but it wasn't broken. We had to be at the theater in 30 minutes, there wasn't enough time to recover from what had just happened! Leo showered quickly as I pulled myself together. 20 minutes after the demonic attack we were out of the door with three heavy record bags weighing us down. We made our way through the crowd and quickly set up. I spent the next three hours in a shocked daze as Leo played one record after another. The music was obscure and powerful and the crowd went wild for it. I felt lighter than I had earlier in the evening, like that misty gloom had dissipated, but I was still unnerved about what I had witnessed. I tried over and over to explain what I saw. I know how I felt and I know what I saw, and I believe that something very evil had attacked us in that room!

After the session, we made our way through the crowds of fans that came just to hear Leo play. There were some pats on the back and thumbs up, and it was the first time since arriving in Estonia that I felt ok. We returned to the hotel, discussing the series of events. Leo couldn't remember anything that happened from the time I went into the bathroom to get ready. He didn't remember the fight we had, or the fact that he picked me up and threw me across the room, which isn't an easy feat, as I am almost 6 feet tall!

Leo confessed that he was feeling really strange when we entered the theater earlier, and that he had attempted to block out whatever it was using his psychic power. I told him that I thought I saw the black magician with the dark eyes in the theater, and Leo also said he thought he saw him, but he didn't want to scare me so he kept it to himself. Leo recited a couple of prayers for protection, and I placed crystals that I packed in my suitcase around the room. Faint light streamed in through the crack between the curtains, as birds chirped, welcoming a new day. We lay in each others arms and Leo held me tighter than he normally would as I drifted off to sleep.

A flyer from that night.

Chapter 23

Turin, the Satanic capital of Italy

Leo and Christy in Turin, Italy February 2011.

We returned home from Estonia the following day, but the events of those days and nights in Tallinn echoed in my mind. I know what I witnessed with my own eyes, but grasping the realization that evil exists and can affect us in such a dramatic way was mind boggling. We both suffered injuries, and the wounds on my knee were proof that energy outside of our own had influenced us in a profound way. It wasn't the first time Leo experienced such an attack, and he seemed to recover much faster than I did. I became afraid to open myself up through meditation. I felt that it wasn't the right thing for me to be doing, so I stopped all meditation practices, focusing on grounding myself, instead. I did continue to work with crystals, concentrating on building a wall of protection around us using the vibration of certain crystals. I also prayed a lot and refrained from watching anything that would upset me like horror movies and any type of music that felt dark. Instead, I would listen to different frequencies that could lift my energy higher. I noticed that when I listened to certain binaural beats, the white light that I had such a hard time envisioning that horrible night in Tallinn, returned. It felt like I was in a battle and I was trying to survive every day against forces I couldn't see. This reality seemed much more frightening than the horror movies that made me squirm as a child.

We were approaching December 2012 when something big was supposed to happen, according to some, anyway. Leo always contended that it was the start, not the end, of seven years of tribulation, when in 2020, contact with alien intelligence could be revealed to the masses in a substantial way. The veil of Isis would be removed, and we would all know the truth, that our life is an imprisoned existence.

Luckily, that period of time was a very busy one for me, and I was able to divert my attention from all the negativity that we had experienced by focusing on the release of Leo's first book in the Italian language. Volume 1 of his *Confessions* series was met with great success in Italy. For the rest of the year, we traveled around doing conferences and Leo promoted his book. One place that we traveled to that stays in my mind is Turin, Italy. It is said to be the Satanic capital of Italy and I would be lying if I said the thought of being in such a dark place like that would affect me, but I put it out of my mind. I couldn't hide, and now that the book was released we would be exposed to even more outside influences. There was a big possibility that Leo could piss off powerful people with his revelations. If we were meant to do this work, we had to have strong protection around us.

Good vibes!

At the time, my esoteric knowledge was very limited. I only began to understand the complexity of hidden knowledge when I began editing Leo's *Confession* series in the English language in 2014. As I mentioned before, Leo's books up until that period were only available in Japanese and Italian. Looking back as I write this, I remember feeling so much confusion. I didn't understand the hierarchy of angels, extra-dimensional beings, and how they related to the alien-UFO experience, until years later.

In May 2012, we were in Turin to attend a big book fair, and were reunited once again with Princess Kaorou, who also released a book with the same publisher. Leo and Kaorou had kept in touch and exchanged publishing favors, a Japanese tradition, and Leo released three more books in Japan through Kaorou's publishing company. After the fallout with Benjamin Fulford, the books that Leo co-wrote with him didn't go into reprint, so Leo was happy to have his work circulating in Japan again.

We were booked for two days at a hotel in the center of town where original artwork of a very dark nature scattered the walls of the lobby and corridors. The walls were painted dark red, and with every turn you found yourself confronted with profoundly disturbing images. A haunting mask depicting Baphomet was mounted just outside the entrance of our room. Every time I passed it, I felt the energy change around me. It was like no matter how hard I tried to push disturbing images of demons and evil out of my mind, the more they would surface to taunt me!

Princess Kaorou was also booked at the same hotel, and it was a funny sight to see her wearing elaborate gowns and jewels, perched delicately on the edge of the divan in the lobby, surrounded by skulls and horned demons. She was accompanied by her two Japanese cameramen, which just added more comedy to the situation.

The morning before returning to Rome, we invited the Princess to accompany us on a tour of the Egyptian museum, which was founded in 1824, and ranks second only the one in Cairo. Leo warned me to proceed with caution and told me to not touch any of the statues or artifacts as the energy is so strong you wouldn't want to come into direct contact with it. I made sure to heed his warning and kept a comfortable distance, as I glided through the galleries studying each of the relics I encountered. The one that stands out the most was Nefertiti, the Egyptian Queen, whose name translates to, *"the beautiful one has come."* She was indeed beautiful and I became transfixed with her regal face, as I scanned her high cheekbones, her missing eye, and her graceful neck.

I felt hypnotized as I felt my imagination transport me back to Ancient Egypt. I swayed on my feet and a rush of cold air swirled around me. I snapped out of my reverie in time to notice the group had wandered into another room of the gallery, and I could hear Leo was going into great detail, explaining the history of a relic to an attentive Princess Kaorou. I hurriedly caught up with the group, taking one last look over my shoulder at Nerfertiti. I could spend hours staring at her.

We ended our visit to Turin and bid farewell to the Princess and her two trusty cameramen with a lot of bowing and promises to see each other again soon.

Leo and Princess Kaorou at the Egyptian Museum in Turin, Italy.

On the way to the train station, Leo became engaged in conversation with the taxi driver, who recognized him from a popular Italian television show called *Mistero*, that had done a segment on the Illuminati. Leo told me later that he recognized the taxi driver as a member of the *Ordo Templi Orientis*, which was a bit ironic, because Leo had exposed so much of the group in his *Confessions* series.

Upon returning to Rome, Leo was booked for another conference that I did not attend. I felt like I had been going non-stop and I needed a break. I decided that the two days that Leo was gone, I would take up painting again. I had used art successfully in the past as a creative outlet, and I felt the urge to paint. One afternoon, I set up my little easel, and using art supplies that had belonged to Leo's father, I began to paint. When I picked up the worn handle of his much loved paintbrush, I could feel the happy energy of Elio surround me. I could sense that he liked that I was painting.

When my father passed on, I had used art to escape my grief, and I could spend hours upon hours lost in my paintings. At first, I painted seascapes, but was later inspired to paint German castles. So, surrounded by all this beautiful energy, I composed my first painting in Italy. I decided to paint Archangel Uriel, I wanted to create something visual that could protect us. I was surprised at how well the painting came out, and I was anxious to show Leo when he returned home.

Leo barely made it through the front door, before I was ushering him into the living room to view my prized painting. He seemed impressed and I beamed as he complimented me over, and over again. I felt so proud that I had produced a work of art that came directly from my heart. He insisted that we have it framed professionally, which he had done the next day, returning home with Uriel surrounded by a beautiful golden frame. I hung it in the stairway so that every time I went up the stairs where the bathroom and bedrooms were, I would pass it. It gave me great comfort to have an angel watching over us that I could see.

I was startled awake by a nightmare one stormy night a couple of weeks later. I had been dreaming of that night in Estonia again. The rain pounded on the rooftop, and with the periodic crash of thunder and bolt of lightning, it was almost impossible for me to fall back to sleep. I looked at the alarm clock on the nightstand, it was almost 3 am, so I decided to get up for a glass of water. On my way to the bathroom, I passed the stairway leading to the first floor, where a skylight in the hall above the stairway led to where on the second landing, I could see Uriel perched with a sword ready to defend me at all costs!

Archangel Uriel Acrylic on paper 2011.

On my return to bed, I passed the stairway again, but this time it was lit up. I peered up and to my astonishment I saw what appeared to be a silver flying disk hovering over the house!

I stood there squinting up through the skylight, trying to figure out what I was seeing. I was bathed in eery silver light and as I looked down at my hands, they appeared to glow!

Oh my God, this is when they beam me up!!

In a panic, I raced back to bed and hid under the blankets. I hugged Leo and he stirred, but he was still fast asleep. The next morning, I told Leo all about the UFOs that came in the night, and he reminded me that there is a place in the hills that is famous for UFO sightings and someone had recently told him they had been abducted. I didn't have a witness to what happened, so it was hard for me to believe that what I saw was real.

I remembered every moment of the experience and decided that maybe it was a sign and took it as that. Perhaps this whole talk of alien encounters was true and they were trying to prepare me for a future event? I really wanted to stay grounded, and so I pushed the whole incident out of mind. I met too many people through Leo that had experienced UFO sightings and abduction experiences and I could feel that it had a negatively effected their energy. The thought of being abducted by evil aliens scared me so much that I didn't want to spend any of time thinking about it. *Where thoughts go, energy flows* was one of my mantra's. I would focus on the beauty that surrounded me even if it killed me!

Chapter 24

Princess Kaorou comes to visit

One morning, Leo received a surprise phone call from Japan. Princess Kaorou was interested in visiting Rome again and asked if Leo could connect her with high level officials of the Vatican that were interested in working together. She wanted to conduct some interviews and attempt to open a dialogue between Japan and the Vatican. Interviews with world leaders is something that she is well-known for, as Newsweek magazine coined her the Edward B. Murrow of Japan. She has interviewed many famous world leaders in the past, such as, Edward M. Kennedy, the Shah of Iran, Mohammad Reza Pahlavi, and Idi Amin.

Leo was also organizing an event called *Contact*, that would be held at Brancaccio castle in Roviano, the village we lived in. She agreed to be a special guest speaker in exchange for his help with the Vatican. Leo spent the rest of the summer meeting with Vatican officials including Antonio Montauro, who was head of a project called *Temple of the Holy Spirit*, in a place called Palestrina. He could connect Kaorou with the right cardinals and bishops that she wished to interview, and because of her special relationship with the dictator of North Korea, they also hoped to initiate a peace project by inviting Kim Jong-Un to the Vatican.

When I heard the idea, I thought it was pretty far-fetched, but I tried to stay positive and supportive and help Leo whenever I could.

Princess Kaoru Nakamaru and Giovanni Tonucci at the time titular archbishop of Torcello—prelate of Loreto and pontifical delegate of the Sanctuary of the what is supposed to be the Holy House of Mary.

In Palestrina near Rome with Princess Kaoru and various Vatican representatives at the Center of the Holy Spirit - Via delle Piagge, 68 - 00036 Palestrina (Roma).

Princess Karou with her translator Haruhiko Yamanouchi, known for his part in *The Wolverine* film, and the Bishop of Palestrina and a couple of Vatican officials.

Leo is having fun with the Princess in Palestrina and the priest seems

to appreciate it.

Farewell dinner for the Princess that I attended with Leo.

Summer 2011 quickly came to an end and I felt sad again. It was always so hard to say goodbye to my son after spending so many summer months together. I tried to not fall into a depression again so I decided to pick up my paint brush. I wouldn't say that anything that I painted was that incredible, but it took my mind to a far away place where sadness couldn't reach me.

I began to mediate, as the experience in Estonia had finally worn off and I felt like I could open myself up again. I missed the peace that meditation gave me, and the sense of calm I experienced in earlier sessions returned like an old friend. Leo continued on his quest to organize another conference on the 2012 subject for the following month and I spent time meditating and painting what I saw. It seemed creating artwork was easier for me after I meditated and my creations became more and more of a mystic nature.

One afternoon, I was home alone, so I decided to meditate. I set the mood by lighting candles, and selected the crystals I would use. I generally would meditate in my bedroom, or in the living room, but this time I decided to use my son's bedroom for my meditation session.

I lay on the bed with special crystals placed on my chakra points, as the scent of candles and incense filled the air. It took me a while to clear my mind, but once I did, I felt a very strong sense of connection. I traveled to another place, where I found myself seated at the end of a long table. After a moment, I noticed there was a female figure seated at the other end of the table, who quickly rose to her feet. To my amazement, I realized that the figure I was looking at was Marilyn Monroe! It was strange to see her in my meditation, as most of the figures I encountered were unfamiliar to me in this dimension. I knew who she was and the tragic way she died, but that was the extent of my connection to her. I admired her beauty, but I would never consider myself a fan. I hadn't seen any of her movies, and never read a book or watched a documentary on her life. Her appearing in my meditation was completely obscure, and I questioned *what she was doing there?*

She rose to her feet and spoke directly to me. There was so much emotion in what she was saying that I could feel her sadness wash over me. She felt that she was had been disgraced by what was said about her after she was *murdered,* and it was all *lies.* I was shown images of the death scene in her bedroom. Bobby

Kennedy was there and a couple of other dark figures. She told me they killed her because she was going to go to the press the following Monday and spill the beans about what was being kept from the public. They were doing crazy things at Area 51, and she had to tell!

She was *very* upset with the way she was killed and how her body was handled. She told me that at one point she was set aside in a broom closet! *The disrespectful heathens!!* I can't describe in words the strong emotions I felt and before I knew it she was gone and I was left with tears streaming down my face.

I tried to grasp what I had just seen. *This was crazy!* Why was she coming to me and saying all of this? I have enough problems of my own, I don't need to take on a disenchanted spirit! Who was I, to Marilyn, I mean *what the heck is the connection?* I slowly rose, wiping my tears away and went downstairs to my laptop.

I looked up everything I could find on the internet about Marilyn's death and there was actually something written about the CIA and a UFO disclosure. I still couldn't understand why she had come to me. *Did she want my help?* I told Leo about my meditation when he returned home and I thought about Marilyn a lot in the next couple of days, it seemed I couldn't escape her. It's as if the energy that I felt during my meditation had followed me into this dimension.

I decided to start a new painting, what ended up being a storyboard of what I thought Marilyn was trying to show me, and that was the beginning of my affair with Marilyn Monroe. I have tried to get rid of her, but she's persistent! From 2012-2016, I completed 20 large paintings, some in oil, some in acrylic, with Marilyn Monroe as my subject. I tried a couple of times to paint something else, but I just didn't feel inspired.

My first charcoal sketch of Marilyn.

It was hard to take pictures of my paintings of Marilyn. Many came out like this, or with orbs all over the picture. This one is really strange!

Part of my storyboard included JFK.

I had a hard time displaying my paintings, or trying to explain them. It made me uncomfortable to hang them where people could see, even though that's what Leo wanted me to do when I completed one. I couldn't explain my far-out artwork to anyone, I can't even explain it to myself! I didn't know why I was painting these images, but besides sharing my latest Marilyn painting on Facebook, that was as far as I wanted to go with publicly displaying them. Maybe I was, and still am, worried that it would be too hard to explain. It seemed I was painting these images for me and for Marilyn and if they are meant to be shown then they will be. For now, they are stored in a room, carefully preserved in case that moment arrives.

The *Contact* conference I mentioned earlier was a success, and the following month *National Geographic* sent a crew to interview Leo on the 2012 subject that had been gaining momentum.

Princess Kaorou conducted the interviews she wanted to conduct, although there was a bit of a scandal in the aftermath of her trip to Italy. The Vatican had named the Princess Special Ambassador to the Vatican for Japan during her visit to Rome, but on her return home she received a surprise visit from Japanese Secret Service, who warned her against going any further with a peace project involving the Vatican and North Korea. She said she was threatened and quickly withdrew, writing an apology note. She gave up her quest for dialogue with the Vatican, as her visit to Rome with Leo as her escort opened her eyes to many truths. In the end, they co-wrote a book together in Japanese and Leo writes about his adventures with Kaorou in Rome in Volume 2, of his *Confessions* series.

On the way to the airport to pick up the Japanese Princess.

Flowers for Princess Kaorou on her arrival to Fiumicino Airport in Rome.

Leo and his cameraman, and the sponsors of the 2012 event, at the airport to greet the Princess.

Chapter 25

It's just politics...

T he *"end of the world"* conference that Leo organized the month before had caused a lot of attention. During that time, he had also released *Confessions* Vol 2. and he was about to release a book about the Pope that was co-written with another author named Enrica Perruchietti. He was asked to participate in a lot of Italian television shows including *Mistero*, the program that I mentioned earlier.

Feeling the 2012 vibe.

He also came in contact with some Italian politicians who encouraged him to run for a seat in parliament. Italy needed a revolution and Leo was just the man to help orchestrate it!

"But how can you trust a politician?" I asked Leo more than once. It seemed he was always bashing the system, how could he then become a part of it? He explained that Italy needed change from the inside out and convinced me that it was something that he had to do. I supported him, even campaigning with him a couple of times to gain votes. Well, it was an interesting experience and we both learned a lot from it. Unfortunately, he didn't win the seat in parliament that he had hoped for but he made contacts with people that pushed him, at the end of the year to participate with the *Forconi* to a revolution in Italy.

Votate Grande Sud con
LEO ZAGAMI candidato
per la Camera dei Deputati
nel Collegio Abruzzo

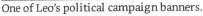

One of Leo's political campaign banners.

Leo and professor Antonio Maria Rinaldi in Rome at Palazzo Ferrajoli, in front of the Italian parliament, interviewed by National TV.

Around November, Leo introduced this project to me and he was convinced that if you gathered enough people you could force change on the government. Leo spent a lot of time away from home snapping pictures of himself with different politicians that were supporting the *Forconi*, or "Pitchforks," a loosely formed movement of anti-government protesters. I had a really bad feeling about a lot of the people that Leo was spending time with. I felt that sinking feeling when he would bring up the names of this person and that during conversation,

and I couldn't help blurting out, *"I don't like that guy,"* but Leo was used to me telling him how I felt, and he basically ignored my warnings.

A huge crowd of over 5,000 gathered *at Piazzale dei Partigiani* in mid-December for the *Forconi* protest and Leo was ushered to the stage to give a speech. He motivated the crowd and everyone cheered when he spoke. I watched on t.v. from home, on the phone with Leo's mother, who watched from her house across the valley. We both agreed that Leo did a great job.

After the protest, many people came up to Leo and patted him on the back to thank him. The following day, Leo posted about the revolution on his Facebook page and unfortunately his publisher and the co-author of the book that was just about to be released didn't share his enthusiasm politically. There was a heated phone call and they warned Leo to drop out of his political endeavors or they would pull his books from the bookshelves and break all of his contracts. Leo is not a person that you can threaten, so in response he dared them to do it. *He wasn't about to be censored by anyone for what he believed in!*

His books were immediately removed from all of the bookshops in Italy and the contract was canceled. Almost simultaneously, he received a call from the producers of *Mistero*, who canceled his next television appearance. This only made Leo fight harder. He felt the media was against him and he was going to do whatever he could to let people know! Leo attended a smaller protest at the same piazza the next week, proudly wearing his grandfather's pin, who was a famous politician in Sicily. I again watched from home, as Leo was worried that it would be too dangerous for me.

Leo gave another speech that was received with a lot of cheers. As he left the stage, a news camera approached him and the crowd closed in. Leo spoke about the protest, and went on to say that the leftist Communist media was censoring him and that they were a bunch of liars and hypocrites. The crowd cheered to a fever pitch, but when Leo tried to continue, the microphone was abruptly snatched from his hand. The crowd booed, and Leo was physically pushed out of the spotlight, he felt something sharp at his back, so he quickly fled the scene, ducking in and out of alleys until he made it back to his car.

"This isn't good," I cried through the telephone line to Leo's mother on the other side of the valley.

"No, it isn't, darling," Leo's mother agreed.

I called Leo to make sure he was okay, and he said he would talk to me when he got home. A few hours later, he burst through the door, talking on his phone as he entered the house, and he didn't hang up for 30 minutes! I anxiously sat staring at him from the couch until he finished his call.

They had censored his books, his television appearances, and now the news media was censoring him as well. So many people witnessed what happened on the news program and supported him, he gained thousands of friends and followers from Italy on Facebook. When we went out together people would stop him in the street and thank him for having the courage to say what they all felt. I felt like something really bad was approaching like a dark cloud again. No matter how Leo tried to turn the negative experience of being censored into a positive one by focusing on changing the government in Italy, I just couldn't jump on board. He would talk to one character in particular, and I would feel such extreme anxiety, I would have to leave the room. Something really bad was about to happen, and there was nothing I could do to stop it!

Trying to protect myself with crystals.

Chapter 26

Has the world gone mad?

A few days later, Leo announced that he had to go to a town about an hour away to attend an important meeting. The person he was meeting and some others, were the same ones that I spoke about earlier. I begged Leo not to go. He reassured me everything would be fine, but I continued on.

"I have a really bad feeling that they are going to do something to you, you are going to be poisoned, please...I beg you...don't go!"

I was in tears and down on my knees, but, unfortunately, he didn't heed my warning, which lead to a series of events that surmounted to the worst experience I have ever endured, even worse than my father's suicide!

Leo in front of the entrance of a Masonic lodge in Arezzo.

Leo returned in the early morning hours to find me waiting up for him, as usual. I always felt such relief when he made it home in one piece from one of his adventures, but this time relief didn't come. As soon as he entered the house I knew there was something wrong with him. He seemed strangely different than the person that left in the late afternoon, several hours earlier. He was agitated and nervous, and paced the floor, recounting the events of the night and how the protests weren't enough, something more had to be done. He was acting very patriotic, but in a crazy way that made me feel really anxious and uneasy. To me, he seemed like he was on something and I told him so. I urged him to go to bed, but he refused. There was too much to do! I looked at his glazed over eyes and felt a sense of doom.

I slunk up to bed on my own that night, but I barely slept. Now and then I would call down to him from the top of the stairs, and he would tell me, *"Five minutes, in five minutes I will come to bed."* He never came to bed that night, and he slept very little in the nights that followed. During the day, he acted completely out of character. I had known him for 5 years at this point, and even in his most heightened state of eccentricity, he was always focused and intelligent. We had so many fights, and I pleaded with him to get help.

I confided in Leo's mother, who also saw the change in Leo. She told me if it got too much for me that she would come and fetch me and I could stay with her, but I felt that abandoning him would be the worst thing I could do, so I stuck it out. It seemed that in the next week, my world turned upside down. *Where was the man I loved so much?* I could barely look at this imposter that called himself Leo! It was like an entity had jumped into his body and taken over, but the experience was not comparable to what happened in Estonia. This was different. He was acting almost like a robot who was being remotely controlled, doing things that were bound to eventually get him arrested, or locked in a nuthouse!

It was almost impossible to enjoy Christmas, but I tried.

For a break one evening, Leo convinced me to go to dinner, as we had been fighting a lot. Sitting in the passenger seat with my arms crossed defensively, we passed through the piazza, to have dinner in another village close by. It was Christmas time, and evening mass was going on. To my surprise, Leo suddenly stopped the car and told me to wait a minute, that he would be right back. He grabbed something from the back of the car and ran into the church. Before I could start to panic, he returned as if nothing had happened. We drove to dinner as I questioned him about what he had done, and he replied, *"Don't worry."*

I found out shortly afterward that he had replaced baby Jesus in the nativity with an evil looking doll someone had given him years ago as a gift. It was meant to be a message to the congregation that they were living a lie, as the priest supported a pedophile ring. He said this as he left the church, to make sure the message was clear. Well, you don't do this kind of thing in a small Roman Catholic village, surrounded by monasteries and churches and devout old ladies!

Leo's mother called and questioned me daily, wanting to know all of the details about the revolution. Who was Leo meeting and what he was doing? I thought it was because she was concerned and trying to help, but unfortunately I had to find out the hard way that nothing appeared as it seemed anymore. There is something wrong with him, I cried over and over. *Please believe me!* Trying to explain this to a sensible British woman was nearly impossible and just left me feeling frustrated. The stress was taking a toll on my health. I hadn't slept and I began losing my hair in clumps. I lost 10 lbs, which was a lot for me and left me feeling weak and frail. It seemed like everyone in the village hated us after what Leo did, and I couldn't bear it!

Leo was avoiding his mother, and so on Sunday, instead of having our afternoon meal together, as we traditionally did, Leo decided to take me out to a restaurant in a really rough area outside of Rome. Sitting at lunch listening to him was horrible for me. When he spoke he rambled, it was like he never stopped talking! He said such bullshit, I just wanted to slap him, and at one point I couldn't take it anymore. I stood up, gathered up Rambo and my purse, and told him I had had enough! *"I want to go back home to America!"* I announced.

I ran out of the restaurant but when I got outside and I looked around, I realized I didn't know where I was! I decided to turn left and as I held Rambo close to me, I ran. I could hear Leo coming after me, so I turned down a gravel road with houses scattered here and there. Distance was gaining between us, but I couldn't escape him! At one point, I felt a force at the center of my back that thrust me forward with such an impact that my feet left the ground. I landed hard on my elbow, ripping my coat and causing a lot of damage to my arm, which eventually I would have to have surgery for. Miraculously, Rambo didn't get hurt.

I don't have time to bleed, a Clint Eastwood quote my dad liked, ran through my mind, as I sprang to my feet. I quickly gathered up Rambo and took off again, but now Leo was right behind me! As I ran past a rickety old house, a young guy without a shirt on was standing in his driveway and stared at me incredulously as I passed. I could hear Leo yelling to the man to stop me, so I screamed in Italian, *"Aiutami, lui e pazzo!!- Help me, he is crazy!!!*

The man disappeared in his garage, and a second later appeared with a shotgun. I ducked behind a large bush trying to catch my breath. Leo said something in rapid Italian and showed the man something he had in his wallet. The guy nodded and to my disbelief, they both started running towards me! I took off back the way I came, but I was going in circles! I didn't know where else to go, so I gave up and stopped running. My elbow hurt, I was tired, and I just wanted this whole charade to end.

We didn't speak much on the way home, but as soon as I had a free moment I called Leo's mother. She said she had been calling me all day. I told her about everything that had happened and she insisted that she would come and get me. I refused, saying I couldn't leave him, and we ended the call with her making me promise to call her if anything else happened. I bandaged my bloody elbow, the damage wasn't just superficial, but I could bend it, and it wasn't broken, so I would survive. So many battles and I always end up getting hurt! I went to bed that night very sad. I cried myself to sleep with the thought that the man I loved was gone forever. Again, I thought about packing my things and returning to America. *I didn't know how to help Leo.*

Chapter 27

8 am wake up call

*B*ang, bang, bang*! I thought I was dreaming at first, but as I opened my eyes and peered at the hazy morning light streaming in through the bedroom window, I realized that it wasn't a dream. *Ohhh, what now???* I thought, as I shook Leo awake.

He sprang out of bed in his pajamas shouting, *"Chi e?"* Who is it? in Italian, and rushed downstairs as I quickly jumped out of bed, throwing on my dressing gown. I stood at the head of the stairs, too afraid to follow Leo down and heard a big crash, as the front door splintered, and then, to our disbelief, Italian police came rushing in! Leo didn't have time to reach the front door, when he was confronted by three large Carabinieri who had invaded our living area! I cautiously descended the staircase and as I passed Archangel Uriel, I begged for protection.

Apparently, there had been *"complaints"* from the neighbors, and Leo was ordered to accompany them. They didn't say where they were taking him, or why.

This was my worst nightmare! They were taking him away! Just like he wrote in his books!

I tried not to let them see me cry, but the tears came automatically. Leo didn't resist them as much as I thought he would, maybe he was still drugged, or maybe they were controlling him remotely to make him more lucid. At that point, I would have believed anything!

Leo went upstairs to dress, and I quickly followed, there was no way I was going to stay down in the living room. Leo tried to call his so-called *friends* that said if this ever happened they would help him. I wasn't surprised when no one answered his calls.

Before I knew what was happening, Leo was escorted out of the broken front door. He reassured me that everything would be fine and not to worry, but I felt frantic! I called Leo's mother and she came right away and told me that in the middle of the night she had received a strange phone call and the person on the phone stated that Leo must be admitted into the hospital because he was poisoned. I wanted to trust Leo's mother so much that I believed what she told me.

We sat in my living room nervously smoking cigarettes as I questioned her over and over about the phone call. Leo wrote about people being made to shut up in this way, and now we were experiencing it first hand. It was an attack to make Leo seem insane so he would be locked away and no longer a threat. No matter what happened in the past week, I knew it wasn't Leo, and it wasn't his fault. *They come like snakes, seducing you with lies!*

I tried to get through the following weeks, but I was like a scared mouse hunched in my dark house, afraid that at any moment they would break the door down again and get me. Every time I went out I would arm myself with crystals, it's all I had, and my faith that the universe had better plans for us than this. The Buddha quote, *The mind is everything, what you think you become*, kept going through my head.

I was always so positive all the time, always smiling, trying to spread happiness. *Look at where it got me.* It didn't feel safe to be here anymore. This revolution that the majority of Italians-didn't give a crap about caused us to lose everything that we worked so hard for in the previous 5 years. It wasn't fair!

Leo fought to be discharged from the hospital, and against much resistance he was finally set free. The situation in Italy was becoming even more tense, and we heard news of other *Forconi* members being forcefully hospitalized or arrested. Leo let me know one afternoon that he wanted to go to America and I couldn't believe my ears! I hadn't been back in 5 years and was so anxious to see my oldest son, who wasn't able to visit due to his job in the military. Maybe something good would come of all this bad!

I didn't know where I wanted to go in America, it seemed nowhere was home now, and since I moved away to Italy my family had scattered all over the country. We decided on California, a place that we both wanted to see. I imagined the warm California sun and the ocean air healing us of everything bad that had happened. I spent a month preparing for the trip, and Leo was able to line up a few interviews in Hollywood. He really wanted his *Confessions* series available in the English language, and he was hoping that he could make the connections that he needed to sign a book deal.

I still received no news about my residence permit, despite constantly checking to see if anything changed from my appeal. It was always the same, I could go on like this for the rest of my life. I was a prisoner in the Italian system that had cost me 5 years of not seeing my family in America. Thank God my youngest son faithfully visited me 2 or 3 times a year, otherwise it would have been unbearable for me.

We decided that we would get married in Las Vegas, so on my return to Italy I wouldn't have all of the problems I faced previously. I could go to the embassy in Los Angeles, file my marriage papers, and maybe then I could obtain my residency permit in Italy. All the planning was really good for me and helped me to pass the remaining days in Italy before our departure for America.

Smiling. Always. Smiling.

Chapter 28

Arrivederci Roma

The weather was gloomy as we gathered our suitcases, and with Rambo in tow, departed for the airport. As I closed and locked the front door of the little apartment we shared, I wished all the sadness and disappointment could be contained, not to follow us another day. With a heavy heart, I remembered when I first arrived 5 years ago, and how happy I was to be free of my marriage. We had been through so much, and with all the trials and tribulations that Leo and I had experienced, I loved him even more. Through the culmination of all of our battles, the bond between us felt even stronger. I felt so sad when he recalled those difficult nights he spent away from me in the hospital. I tried to imagine how horrible it would be to be sane, locked away with the insane, forced to take medicine that actually facilitated the whole effect. I swallowed hard and wiped away my tears, as I turned the key in the lock, pushing the terrible memories away.

On the way to the airport.

As I sat in the backseat of Leo's mother's car on the way to the airport, I pulled a tarot card from my Goddess Deck that I kept in my purse, *Don't worry, everything is going to be fine,* it read. It was like a comforting hug from the universe letting me know that all would be fine again. I counted so much on signs like these, and made sure to listen, instead of questioning. There was so much that happened in the past years that couldn't be explained, except to say it was beyond my realm of understanding. We were on our way to America, to a new place and a new adventure. I tried to put the trauma of the past months behind me, but the experience that I had endured showed not only on the inside, but on the outside as well. Life is full of lessons, and if we don't learn from them, we tend to repeat them. I wanted to make sure that we both learned from this ordeal, even if it meant not trusting people anymore.

I carried this card with me for 3 months. Goddess Guidance Oracle Deck by Doreen Virtue.

The plane slowly ascended through the oppressive clouds that covered Rome, and then there was bright sunshine, it was as if the sun appeared just for me. I smiled as I settled in my seat, and with Leo safely buckled in beside me, I finally felt like everything was going to be okay. We had escaped, and we would never make the same mistakes again. I closed my eyes and dreamed of holding my sons in my arms. I imagined being in America, my home, the place I never realized I would miss so much, until my freedom was taken away from me...

Chapter 29

Sympathy for the Devil

I barely slept on the plane, and I was beginning to feel jittery when we landed in California. Our rental car was an automatic, so I had to drive from Los Angeles to Long Beach, where we were staying. I never liked driving, and it had been 5 years since I had been behind the wheel of a car. I was going to be tested in L.A. traffic, but I had to do it, so I did.

We made it to Long Beach around 11 pm and found our keys waiting for us, just as prearranged. We would be staying in a beautiful penthouse apartment in the Art District of Long Beach, and we couldn't be more pleased with our choice. There was a special key to reach the penthouse from the elevator, which made it feel very secure and safe. We were perched high above the city, able to observe our surroundings from the safety of our rooftop balcony.

We walked around the apartment, viewing all of the obscure artwork that decorated the walls, that was more to Leo's taste, than my own. To my surprise, the long hallway that led to the bedroom, that was not visible in the pictures I viewed on the internet, was dedicated to Marilyn Monroe and JFK! Every morning I was greeted with large black and white framed photographs of Marilyn. I felt it was her way of telling me we were safe and welcome, and maybe another message from the universe to let me know that everything was going to be okay.

Marilyn greeted me when I walked into the Long beach penthouse.

We quickly got used to the laid back, fun and sun atmosphere of California. We were in a city, surrounded by large buildings, but in a style much different than New York. I enjoyed my morning coffee from the balcony, as I peered down at all the action going on below. My very first morning in California I heard a man on the corner of our street announcing Armageddon. There was always something going on and the helicopters that flew overhead added to the ambiance. I could just imagine what the next couple of months would have in store for us. Leo was feeling very laid back and happy, it seemed that the ghosts of the past two months weren't haunting him, which was good. He was focused on moving forward, and I liked that. I didn't want to dwell in the past, I just wanted to forget it all, and the drastic change of scenery was really helping.

We are relieved to be out of Italy, and excited to be in California!

Leo loves American supermarkets.

Palm trees and sunshine, looking up from the smoothie shop across the street from our penthouse condo in Long Beach, California.

News leaked out in the alternative media that Leo had been locked up, and I received a few questions from people on Facebook asking if we were ok. I didn't know how to explain in a few sentences, or a paragraph, what had happened, nor did I feel the urge to do so. It was unbelievable to my own ears, so I couldn't imagine anyone else believing it. Most of all, I didn't want to burden anyone with my problems. I shared my Facebook with under two hundred people, and I continued to post positive antidotes as if nothing had happened. My youngest son spent his spring break, and a month of his summer break from college with us. It was such a relief when he only had to fly a couple of hours, instead of across the Atlantic.

Tomorrow was a big day. Leo was meeting Sean Stone, the son of Oliver Stone, to be a guest on his show called *Buzzsaw*. The studio was located in downtown Beverly Hills, and we would be having breakfast together before filming. It was a great opportunity for Leo, and in the end with the help of Sean, he was able to sign a book deal, and I was able to see Marilyn's star!

Chapter 30

Beverly Hills 90210

I was nervous about my appearance the morning that we drove to L.A., but I did my best to artfully apply my makeup and chose my outfit carefully, but every time I caught a glimpse of my reflection, I felt a sinking feeling. There was nothing more that I could do. I tried to carry myself with grace, although inside I felt horrible. I was in Hollywood, the glamour capital of the world, and I felt far from my best. We met at a trendy outdoor café, and as we sat at a corner table, I observed the people around me. It was only 9 am, but the place was packed, and surprisingly I didn't see any of the *"Hollywood types"* I expected. It seemed most were normal people, eating breakfast at an outrageously priced café in the center of Beverly Hills in hopes of spotting their favorite stars. Leo was dressed in his usual black suit and tie and received more than a few quizzical looks from the other diners in the restaurant.

Tony at Urth Café in Beverly Hill

The interview was a success! I was so proud of Leo, who spoke with such poise and intelligence. I could tell that Sean was impressed, and we ended up meeting him two more times, as he attempted to connect us to his friends in Hollywood, who he thought would be interested in financing the big job of translating the books from Italian. The show would air that night at 7 pm, so we rushed back to Long Beach in plenty of time. As we were preparing for the show, I noticed that Rambo was acting agitated, and at one point ran into the back bedroom. Leo got up and followed, asking him what was wrong along the way. As my son and I sat at the kitchen counter, the floor seemed to sway beneath us. For a moment, I thought I was having a dizzy spell, maybe being out in the sunshine all day was affecting me? The sway continued, and then Leo announced from the other room, *"Earthquake!!!"*

Live from the set of *Buzzsaw*.

My son and I stared at each other in disbelief! This was the worst place to be in an earthquake, we were surrounded by glass windows! The ground continued to sway, as if on rollers, as we made our way to the small laundry room that was nothing more than a closet. The three of us huddled together and anxiously waited for the swaying to stop. I experienced earthquakes in Rome and Tokyo, but this was the strongest one I had ever felt. After a couple of minutes, the swaying finally stopped, and as we exited the laundry room, we could hear car alarms going off and people speaking in the street far below.

We immediately switched on the news, and it was confirmed that we had just experienced a 5.4 earthquake. I was terrified that this was just the beginning, and there would be another bigger one, but we only felt some small aftershocks, and luckily no damage occurred. We thought about escaping to Italy, but quickly came to our senses. I would rather experience an earthquake like this every day than go back there!

With all the excitement, we almost missed Leo's debut on *Buzzsaw*, but caught it just in time. Immediately afterward, Leo received hundreds and hundreds of Facebook requests. Some of those friend requests filtered into my Facebook profile, but I ignored them. I didn't need any more Facebook friends.

The show was a hit! One of Leo's best interviews. You can find Illuminati, Pope Francis and the Dark Side with Leo Zagami on youtube https://www.youtube.com/watch?v=vf7IP8lffl8

In the following weeks, Leo spent a lot of time on the phone with Brad, his new publisher in San Francisco. There wasn't anyone available that could translate the books, and the complicated subject matter didn't help the situation. In the end, we all decided on using an automated translator, and Leo would have to go through and correct it afterward. Easier said than done, but I will discuss that more in detail later.

We utilized our time in America wisely. We knew we couldn't stay more than three months, not only because Leo would have to go back, but because of the expense! We had splurged on the penthouse apartment and the rental car, slowly draining the small amount we managed to save in the past few years. Everything we did seemed to cost so much money, we would have to make it up somehow. Leo didn't have anything happening in Italy anymore, so this book deal was our only chance. We were grateful for the opportunity, it seemed like the universe was giving us a break.

Chapter 31

Going to the Chapel of Love

Leo expressed such a strong desire to get married in Las Vegas by Elvis Presley that I couldn't refuse. I spent time searching online and found the iconic Graceland Chapel, located in an older section of Las Vegas, and booked our wedding. I didn't know what to wear but decided on a 1960s style short white sequin dress. Not very traditional, but for a wedding in Las Vegas, it seemed suitable.

Graceland Chapel, Las Vegas. We were married on May 1st. which is also the day Elvis married Priscilla, and of course it's the birthday of the Illuminati, and Beltane.

We woke up in the early hours of the morning on May 1st, and quickly prepared for our short journey of a few hours through the desert of Nevada, to Las Vegas. It was over 100 degrees that day, and as we edged closer to our destination, the temperature gauge in the car, rose. Leo was paranoid that we would get stuck in the desert, like a bad horror movie, so we didn't stop at all along the way. I was entertained by the strange sites we passed, some looked like abandoned Hollywood movie sets. When we approached Las Vegas, I expected to see the iconic sign you see in movies, but we were greeted by a carnival of buildings and amusement rides that reminded me of Orlando. The GPS led us to the Four Seasons Hotel, chosen by me, because they didn't have any slot machines in the lobby and they accepted dogs. I stared up at the beautiful building and the ones surrounding it and felt star struck.

We checked in, but didn't have time to relax, we had to find the courthouse so we could register our marriage before the cere-mony. I placed Rambo on the hotel bed and filled his bowls with food and water. He could be completely unpredictable and de-cide to bark as soon as we closed the door. I promised him I would be right back and cautiously closing the door behind me. I hesitated with my ear pressed against the door for a few sec-onds, in case he started barking, but all was silent in the room. Leo hurried me along, and armed with GPS, we made our way to the courthouse.

Standing in line, we were surrounded by the most eccentric characters imaginable, who made us seem normal, if you could imagine! Leo's eyes were huge as he took it all in. *He is going to talk about this forever*, I thought to myself, as I watched him watching everyone around him. One guy at the window was ar-guing with the clerk because he couldn't remember if this was his 5th or 6th wedding, and asked if annulments count? I knew Leo was making eyebrows that would send me into a fit of gig-gles, so I bit my lip and stared straight ahead until it was our turn. It took less than two minutes...sign here...sign here...and *voila*....you are now Mr. and Mrs. Leo Zagami, just like that! I stared at the document in disbelief as we exited into the blazing hot sun.

The Four Seasons, Las Vegas.

We arrived back to the hotel in record time, the ceremony would be at 8 that evening, and it was only 5. We ordered an elaborate dinner from room service and I took a long bath as I sipped champagne and daydreamed about our wedding.

∞∞∞

The time flew by, and before I knew it, it was time to head to Graceland Chapel. I repeated the earlier procedure with Rambo, making sure that he seemed fine before we left. We hoped that he would be able to join us for the ceremony, but we weren't able to arrange it, and were forced to leave him in the room. We called a taxi, we only had 30 minutes to get to the chapel, but the driver got lost and we nearly missed our appointment! We rushed in and were asked for our documents.

We even bought Rambo a tuxedo for the occasion, but unfortunately we were forced to leave him in the hotel room.

The chapel was as tacky as I thought it would be, but charming at the same time. Elvis walked me down the aisle, and he was a great Elvis indeed! Did I mention that my father looked like Elvis, so it was kind of like having dad there, in a way. I tried not to swoon while he serenaded us with two songs, and plenty of photos were snapped. At the end of the ceremony, we all danced to *Viva Las Vegas*, and that was pretty hilarious! I bought a cake and it was waiting for me in a little box when we exited.

Leo had arranged for the taxi driver to wait for us, and there he was, patiently waiting when we exited the chapel. As we entered the taxi Leo turned his phone on, and to my surprise ,there was a message from the front desk of the Four Seasons!

It had to be about Rambo. Leo tried to return the call without success, which left me anxious the whole ride home. We pulled up to the hotel and Leo made his way to the front desk, as I ran for the elevators, balancing my wedding cake as best I could. I slowly ascended to the 44th floor, losing my shoe as I ran down the corridor to our room. I ran back to fetch it, and could hear fierce barking coming from down the hall. I was relieved to hear him, that meant he was okay. As I fumbled to put my electronic key in the slot of the door, it opened quickly from inside, and I was face to face with a frightened Mexican man.

"You're here!"

"Oh my God! Is he okay?" I asked breathlessly as I picked Rambo up.

"He has been barking so the manager asked us to take him for a walk, but he won't let us near him!"

For the first time I noticed a second Mexican guy sitting on the edge of the bed, trying to persuade Rambo to put on his collar. I always removed it when I left him alone for fear it could get caught on something.

"Gucci doesn't like us, he's vicious," the second guy exclaimed.

"First of all, his name is Rambo, not Gucci, and secondly he doesn't like strangers."

"Ohhh hahaha, that is why he didn't come, we were calling him Gucci, as he pointed to the tag on his collar."

"Sorry, we were gone less than an hour, we were getting married," as I showed him the cake box.

They quickly retreated, congratulating me on the way out, as I thanked them for their help. *"Oh Rambo! You are so naughty!"*

At that moment, Leo arrived, and we laughed at the situation. We decided we would just have drinks by the pool, and then return to the room. We talked briefly about seeing a show, but that was impossible with Rambo, he was the boss, and we would be spending the rest of the evening with him!

I sat by the pool admiring my sequin dress in the moonlight, with Rambo plopped on my lap. I couldn't believe we were now husband and wife! Maybe it was my imagination, but I felt different, like the bond we shared was even stronger now.

My wedding day by Christy, Acrylic on paper 2014.

Chapter 32

Mission Accomplished!

We ate our sickeningly sweet wedding cake for breakfast that morning, before heading out on our journey back to California. I felt excited at the thought that because we were married, I could finally get my Italian residency, after all these years. In the back of my mind, I still worried that I would get lost in the system, and unfortunately, it took two more years for me to receive my *permesso di soggiorno*, but not without the help of one of Leo's friends, who knew someone that worked in the office where my documents were held. My file had been placed in what surmounted to a dead file drawer, because it would have never escaped if someone hadn't literally rescued it!

It was 104 degrees as we bid farewell to Las Vegas. I tried my luck at a slot machine, while Leo filled up at a gas station on the way out, and that was the extent of my Las Vegas gambling experience. I didn't win at the slots, but on the way home, luck was definitely with us in other ways, as a wooden bridge collapsed an hour after we passed under it. The highway was blocked for several hours, and we quickly switched on the television when we arrived home, relieved it wasn't us stuck in our hot car, anxiously waiting for debris to be removed from the road. The last month in California was spent sightseeing and I was really anxious to see Hollywood, so one day we decided we would check it out. It was a surreal feeling to see the famous Hollywood sign perched high in the hills.

I have to admit that I felt Marilyn with me that day. We wandered Hollywood Blvd, admiring the Walk of Fame along the way. I was thrilled to spot Marilyn's star without the help of a map. We walked up and down taking in all the characters. I have been lucky in my life to have the opportunity to travel to interesting places, and Hollywood wins hands down for being the most bizarre.

I wanted a hamburger and a milkshake for lunch, so we popped into the Hard Rock Café. I loved to see Leo so happy, and was proud that he found happiness with me in America. I wished we could afford to stay, so he could get his green card and become an American Citizen. Maybe that is what the future has in store for us, who knows? For now, we were here, determined to enjoy every moment.

Leo on Hollywood Blvd.

My youngest son arrived for the last couple of weeks in California, and since he decided he wouldn't be traveling to Italy again
until winter break, we tried to make the most of the little time
we had together. We spent a day visiting Venice Beach, another
place that I was anxious to see. I was a little bit disappointed
when we got there, as it wasn't what I expected. There were
plenty of mystics around, but the shops along the boardwalk
and the scattered vendors seemed too commercial, and a lot of
the originality that made it special had faded in time.

Leo and Tony in Venice Beach June 2014.

The days seemed to fly by, and before I knew it, it was time to pack our suitcases and return to Italy. The summer was just beginning in California, it didn't seem fair we had to leave and miss it. We were gone three months, but it wasn't enough time to erase the bad memories of all the unfortunate experiences in Italy. I cringed when I imagined returning to that little apartment with the ghosts waiting, ready to haunt me again. I felt a lot more clear-headed in California and never felt the depression that I often felt in Italy. I guess it's normal to be home sick, I tried to convince myself, as I stuffed the last of my clothes into my suitcase.

Chapter 33

Ciao Roma!

As we touched down in Rome, we were greeted with sunshine and blue skies. I remembered how everything felt so gloomy and dead when we left, and I was relieved to see that Italy had sprung back to life while we were away. I think we both felt a sense of doom at the prospect of returning to Roviano, *but what choice did we have?* Leo asked a few friends to scout apartments in our price range, but nothing materialized, so we were pretty much stuck. I tried to be positive, and on the way home I attempted to lift our melancoly mood by reliving good times in California. Leo forced a smile, but I could tell he was just as anxious as I was to be back.

It was lunchtime when we slowly pulled up to our two-story apartment. I let out a sigh of relief as I scanned the piazza, and the road leading up to our apartment, *there wasn't a soul around.* Leo didn't tell anyone that he was back in Italy and for the first month we stayed inside. The summer heat finally arrived and we couldn't hide in our stifling apartment anymore, so life returned to normal, I guess. I had to stop worrying about what people thought. I was determined to focus on good things that would help us to get out of the bad living situation we were in.

Back in Roviano.

Leo was able to relaunch his Italian books with another publisher, releasing new updated versions of his *Confessions* series. We had a five-book project with *CCC publishing*, that also kept us busy, which I think was healthy for both of us. Leo attempted to figure out the automated translation, which was a slow, painstaking experience. I often thought it would have been easier if he had just translated it himself. I edited what Leo translated, which proved to be just as difficult of a task. It took 6 months of work, sometimes 12 hours a day, to translate the first book, Pope Francis the last Pope. Thankfully, it was a small book of only 200 pages.

Leo warned me that the *Confessions* trilogy was going to be really difficult to translate and edit, and was that ever an understatement! It seemed that as soon as we finished one book, another one was waiting for us. It was exciting for me to read Leo's work in English. I learned a lot in the years that followed, about secret societies, Freemasons, ritual magic, Satanists, the Vatican...I can go on and on. When Leo would bring up certain topics, I was proud that I could comment now, instead of just listening and not really understanding what he was talking about. As I write this in the spring of 2017, we await the release of Leo's fourth book, *Confessions of an Illuminati Volume 3,* my favorite of the series so far. Leo is working on a new book in English that he is really proud of, (VOl. 6.66) that I will publish on my own, somehow, but we have to finish the 5 book deal first.

Leo speaking at a book conference in late 2014. Even in 2017, he is still censored from mainstream Italian media and his Italian books aren't found on the shelves of the big bookshops any longer. God bless America, where freedom of speech still prevails, despite so many things being wrong with the system.

Leo's books can now only be found in small bookshops around Italy. Prior to the sabotage, his books were found in the large commercial bookshops.

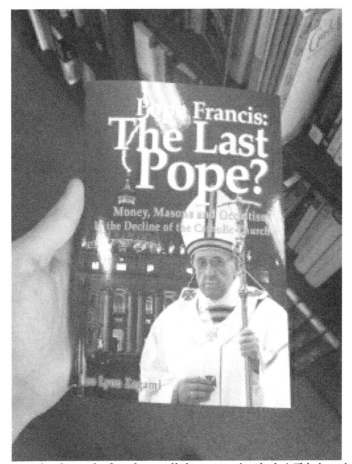

Leo's books can be found even all the way up in Alaska! This is a pic
my son Nick took at Barnes and Noble in Fairbanks, Alaska.

The people that tried to destroy Leo's life all disappeared, and
taking my advice (*for once*) he approached any new connection
with caution. If I felt that something wasn't right about a person, he would listen to me. (*Wow!*) I was right countless times
before, and began to realize that maybe the gift I have is meant
for the purpose of keeping us out of danger. I was like Scully
from *Xfiles*! Remember how she always rescued Mulder at the
last critical moment?

My first magic wand made of copper and quartz burned a hole in the dresser where I kept it, because it was so hot after I used it. I had to Wrap it in cloth, but eventually the whole wand bent and warped.

Shungite and Orgonite pyramids.

Chapter 34

Adventures in Rome with Alex Jones

Although Leo found another publisher in Italy to release the new updated versions of his trilogy, unfortunately, he continued to confront censorship by the left-wing media. As much as he tried, the big bookshops in Italy refused to carry his books, which was a big blow to sales. He tried many times to return to television to promote his work with no luck. It felt like a hopeless cause, so we focused on promoting the books in English instead. In late summer of 2015, we heard news that Alex Jones was visiting Rome. Leo followed the Infowars website, and when Pope Francis and the Vatican were mentioned, it seemed that the information was coming straight from Leo's book, Pope Francis The Last Pope? We thought about going to Rome, but it was August, the hottest month of the year, and we weren't very motivated to do anything more than try to stay cool.

One afternoon, on the way to a leisurely lunch, Leo decided to send a message to Sean Stone, to see if there was a way he could connect Leo with Alex and his team in Rome. When we finally arrived home later that afternoon, we were surprised to see three emails from the producers of *Infowars*! Alex was anxious to talk to Leo, and on their last day in Rome, they said it was like Leo magically appeared. They wanted to meet him in 2 hours at the obelisk to interview him about different subjects concerning the Vatican.

Rome, Italy.

My son was leaving for America in a couple of days, so I stayed home and spent the evening with him, as Leo departed for his adventure. We waited for Leo's phone call, anxious to hear how everything was going. One, two, three hours passed. I tried to reassure myself that everything was fine. A couple of more hours passed, when finally my mobile phone rang.

"Hello? Where are you?" I anxiously asked.

"Christy! How are you?" the familiar voice boomed at the other end of the line.

"Alex?"

Leo asked Alex Jones to call me as a joke and we had a funny conversation, before he handed the phone to Leo, promising to meet each other in the future. Leo said everything was going great and that they were on a dinner break. He told me not to wait for up for him because he didn't know how long everything would take, but of course I would!

That evening and into the night, Leo and the *Infowars* team filmed a spectacular documentary that can be found on Youtube and the *Infowars* website. Leo had access to places and information that impressed Alex, and he became a regular on the Infowars show for the next couple of months. The exposure to a bigger audience really helped book sales, and it was exciting to hear that more people were reading Leo's books. A few months later, Leo was asked to be interviewed for a documentary filmed in Rome, called The *Unholy See,* by a friend of Alex's named Steven Quayle. When offered money for his interview, Leo asked that he could promote his books instead. Timothy Alberino and his team arrived at the Vatican, in a similar fashion as the *Infowars* crew, and Leo escorted them to places they had only heard existed. There was a lot of information exposed that made the *GenSix* team nervous, and on returning to the United States, Leo was surprised to receive a frantic email from Tim, stating that he and his family were in danger, and that there was an attempt on his life!

Leo with Alex Jones in Rome August 2014.

You can watch Leo's documentary on Infowars *entitled Demonic Possession of the Vatican exposed*: https://www.youtube.com/watch?v=fc99vUS_PZE

Leo was sympathetic, but after dealing with the same opposition himself, he knew there wasn't much he could do to help.

It could be a message from the Vatican to stay quiet, but if they wanted Tim and his family dead, they would have succeeded. Most likely it was a message to scare them into not publishing the documentary. They were courageous, and published the documentary anyway, which is available online for purchase. People are opening their eyes to the truths Leo exposes in his books, and not just so-called conspiracy theorists. You always hear that knowledge is key, and it's great that humanity is more aware. I am happy that I understand so much more than I used to.

Leo at the Jesuit headquarters near the Vatican, with Timothy Alberino, filming *The Unholy See*.

Leo didn't want to be paid, he only asked to promote his book *Confessions of an Illuminati Volume 1* as compensation for his time.

Chapter 35

Turbulent times realized

As we approach the end of this book, the stories are becoming more apocalyptic, a *direct reflection of the times we are living in.* Every day you turn on the news to hear about yet another terror attack. I have to admit that I was a little worried when Leo was asked to play in Berlin in February 2017. I lived on an Army base in Germany when I was a child, and remember a field trip to "Checkpoint Charlie" to see the Berlin Wall. My heart raced as I scanned the graffiti-strewn wall, as I wondered what life was like on the other side. Were they so different than other Germans?

On the long ride back to Southern Bavaria, I sketched pictures in my notebook of what I imagined life was like in Eastern Germany. Most of my artwork featured aliens mixed in with Eastern Germans. On the taxi ride from the airport to our hotel, I noticed that the buildings lacked the charm of Southern Germany and Bavaria, there wasn't a picture house or window box in sight. It was even more industrial than I imagined it to be, and the architecture reminded me of military base housing. Thankfully, the hotel was very nice, close to the club, and Berliners were much friendlier than Romans!

Grey skies welcomed us to Berlin in February 2017.

I lived on an Army base in Germany when I was a child, and I remember a field trip to "Checkpoint Charlie" to see the Berlin Wall. My heart raced as I scanned the graffiti-strewn wall, wondering what life was like on the other side. Were they so different than other Germans? On the long ride back to Southern Bavaria, I sketched pictures in my notebook of what I imagined life was like in Eastern Germany. Most of my artwork featured aliens mixed in with the Eastern Germans. On the taxi ride from the airport to our hotel, I noticed that the buildings lacked the charm of Southern Germany and Bavaria, there wasn't a picture house or window box in sight. It was even more industrial than I imagined it to be, and the architecture reminded me of military base housing. Thankfully, the hotel was very nice, close to the club.

Leo with the club organizers outside our hotel. Leo gave them a gift of
Vinyl, they seem pretty happy.

The club was located in a warehouse, where Leo was booked to
play from 3-6 am. We shared dinner with the organizers of the
event, a group of young Italians living in Berlin. The mood was
light and fun and put me at ease. After dinner, we headed back
to the hotel and spent time in the lobby bar where we drank
big mugs of beer and I practiced the German I remembered from
grade school.

2:30 am finally approached, and we headed for the club, lugging
three bags of vinyl down to the taxi stand. We could see and
hear the club from the hotel, but there was no way we would
be able to make it without a ride. The club was packed when
we pulled up in the taxi, and not to stereotype, but everyone
looked like Nazi's to me! We made our way to the DJ booth, and
were warmly greeted by the other DJ's. I breathed a sigh of relief
as I put my heavy record bag down, and Leo prepared for his first
set.

The room we were playing in was on the ground level, which just added to the whole industrial effect. This is going to be an experience, I thought to myself, as I fiddled with the video camera on my phone. An hour went by, as I filmed Leo's first set to post on Youtube and Facebook. Unfortunately, I wasn't paying much attention to what was going on around me, or the man that kept trying to speak German in my ear. I continued to ignore him, but I could see that Leo noticed, and was becoming distracted and agitated.

I muttered, *"I don't speak German, sorry."*

He then asked, *"Where are you from?"*

I said *"America,"* and that is when I looked up for the first time to see that I was was face to face with a Muslim man. He was about 24 years old and smoking a joint. When he heard America his smile faded, and his face became dark.

 "America? I spit on America." And then to my amazement he actually spit on the floor in front of me!

"You know where I am from? Morocco," he proudly stated before I could answer.

At that point, he pulled up the sleeve of his colorful sweater, and with his lighter, he illuminated his forearm, so I could see the tattoo of a bird with spread wings and a red star. I had no idea what it meant, but it couldn't be good. Sweater guy looked at me with disgust and then he stormed off! I stood there in shock as I watched him disappear into the red smoke of the club.

Where was he going, to get bombs?

Oh god, my worst fears were realized in that brief moment of exchange. I started to sweat and looked over at Leo, who was concentrating intently on his DJ set. Once he started playing it was impossible to get his attention. I scanned the room, and spotted one of the organizers out on the dance floor so I quickly pulled her aside so I could tell her what happened.

She also had noticed the guy that I described and told me he gave her the creeps.

"What should we do?" I asked.

"He didn't threaten you so...just wait and see what happens," she cooly replied.

"Wait and see what happens!!" I exclaimed.

"I think you need a shot!" she announced.

I didn't have time to tell Leo I was leaving, but I sent him a mind message that I was going to get him water, and he nodded to me as I took the girl's hand and was blindly led through thick red smoke and a maze of twists and turns that led to the bar upstairs. It reminded me of a Halloween horror ride, where now and then a spooky guy would jump out of the shadows and try to talk to me. I ordered a water for Leo and anxiously looked around for sweater guy. The DJ girl was taking a lot of time chatting and flirting around the bar, and as the minutes passed I became more anxious. I needed to get back to Leo, but there was no way I could find my way on my own, *I needed her.*

The minutes felt like hours as I waited patiently to do my shot and get the heck out of there. Finally, she was ready to go back, so I took her hand and she led me out of the bar and back to the room Leo was playing in. He looked up and I could see he was relieved to see me, he must have been really worried! I quickly apologized and gave him his water.

Quite unexpectedly, Leo directed me to the left side of him, where the DJ booth was closed off in an L shape. I guess now I couldn't wander off again. I felt safer, but as I scanned the room I noticed that there wasn't a visible exit anywhere. You basically had to go back up the stairs we came down, which were really narrow and precarious.

It was 5 am, and Leo had one more hour to play. The room was packed with people, everyone crammed in shoulder to shoulder. If sweater guy appeared with a bomb now, we were doomed! I decided our best bet would be to get under the DJ booth, as there was no escaping this place in an emergency.

I called on all the archangels for protection and envisioned white light surrounding first me, then Leo, then the DJ booth and then extending the light around the entire club. I asked God to please protect us and all the innocent people, *please let us get through this night safely!*

About 5:45 am I was scanning the dance floor for the hundredth time, and finally spotted sweater guy. He just stood there, not dancing, not really interacting with anyone. He caught me looking at him and winked at me, as I quickly looked away, a rush of fear washing over me.

I looked over at Leo who was putting the last record on for his final song of the night. It was a favorite that got everyone singing and dancing. We just had a little while longer and then we could escape. I had to play it cool. If anything happened I would take control and throw Leo under the DJ booth (*I watched too much Charlie's Angel's as a kid.*) I looked at the time, it was 6:05 am, and I was relieved to see the DJ that followed Leo, approaching.

Leo finally turned to me, after three hours, and asked:

"How was it?"

"Oh just wonderful," I replied...

He could hear the sarcasm in my voice and asked if I was okay.

"We need to get out of here, NOW. I will explain later," as I quickly gathered up the last of the vinyl records scattered about.

We said our goodbyes and worked our way through a maze of pipes, broken boxes, and wrought iron. I tried to lead Leo out of the club, but we ended up getting lost, going around in circles before we finally found the inconspicuous exit. I suspected the taxi driver was shooting up drugs right before we approached his car...but I didn't care. I wanted to get as far away from this place as I could, even if it was across the street and around the corner from our hotel and a drugged up taxi driver was taking us there. I explained to Leo what happened, and he agreed that it was a bad situation.

We learned the next day, when we had more time to sightsee, that we were right next to the Muslim quarter of Berlin. *You can't really love thy neighbor when thy neighbor hates you and wants to blow you up or chop off your head!* That is the reality of the world we are living in. I vowed that I would never put myself in that kind of situation again, especially if we return to Berlin. I will pay attention to everything that is going on around me, and I will always look for an exit if I am in a closed off place like that with a bunch of people. We were spared from something horrible, I know that in my heart. *Angels were protecting us once again.*

Chapter 36

Alien Mountain

It was July 2016, and we were in the middle of another infernal Italian summer. The conditions in the apartment we had shared for so many years were quickly deteriorating. The neighbors constantly harassed us, and my day generally began with the sound of swears in Italian from the horrid women who lived below us that would do anything she could to try to make our lives as miserable as hers. In the evening, a toxic odor would rise from her house, and I felt that we were slowly being poisoned to death.

"Maybe they have a meth lab next to their wine cellar," I half joked to Leo one afternoon as I covered my mouth and nose with a handkerchief.

"We got to get the hell out of here," Leo replied. I nodded my head, but I didn't feel very hopeful. We had been saying that for years.

One day, out of the blue, an acquaintance of Leo's mentioned a house that was for rent in the mountains of Subiaco. It had all the requirements that we were looking for, and after Leo described it, I wanted to see it for myself!

One sweltering summer afternoon in July we made an appointment to meet with the owners of the house, a pleasant older couple in their late sixties. I couldn't contain my excitement as we drove away from the familiar landscape of the *Valley of Tears* where I had been living since 2009. We made our way through the town of Subiaco, the hillsides littered with ancient monasteries and churches. We turned off the main road and slowly began driving up a mountain. We passed olive groves and quaint houses that reminded me of Germany, as the road twisted and turned up, and up.

The main road narrowed to a white dirt road and I began to wonder how isolated this place was? Before I could wonder anymore, our future home came into view. It had the feeling of an estate, as the big wrought iron gate slowly opened like the arms of an old friend, greeting us as we approached. We drove through and made our way down the driveway to the front of the house. The charming villa with its characteristic Italian red tile roof was set against a flourish of nature. Birds chirped, butterflies fluttered and bees buzzed among the green fields of wild flowers. Surrounded by majestic mountains speckled with little villages in the distance, I drew in a deep breath of fresh mountain air and tried to take it all in.

I imagined cooking grand meals in the cozy sit-in kitchen with its rustic fireplace tucked in the corner. A beautiful terrace opened off of the kitchen that looked out onto a huge backyard. There was a house in the distance so we weren't totally isolated, but we wouldn't be crammed in like sardines like we were in Roviano. I finally had space to breathe! I imagined meditating in the early morning hours, and evenings spent sitting with Leo on the little wicker sofa drinking tea and talking about life.

In the master bedroom, french doors opened onto a huge field of flowers and trees. As I stepped out onto the balcony, I noticed her for the first time. A statue of the Holy Mary was facing our house! This was a good sign!

We quickly settled into our new place in the fall of 2017. It didn't take long to get used to the silent bliss of country life. Every morning I took long walks with Rambo, and I got to know the Virgin Mary up close. It didn't take long to realize that the whole area was magical! To the right of the Holy Mary, and our house, stood a small mountain that I was drawn to look at. I named it Alien Mountain.

Alien mountain. Is it a stargate? Time will tell.

Leo said that there was an abduction in the late 60s of a farmer working in the fields near the villa and Alien Mountain. The farmer disappeared for four days, and when he reappeared and told his story he was swiftly taken to a nuthouse. After a couple of days the doctors realized that he was indeed not crazy, but urged him to not repeat his story. Word did get around, and the farmer was bombarded with questions from scientists and UFO experts for years.

Leo reminded me that he told me about the story of the farmer when we lived in Roviano. Many years ago, I had been staring out of the window at the moon from Tony's room, where the village of Cineto can be seen at a distance. Cineto is actually right below where we live now, and for seven years I imagined there was a UFO base over there! I actually had the idea that the UFO I saw way back in 2011 came from there!

Leo heard that Franco, the farmer who was abducted owned a bar in Vignola, the little village at the bottom of the road that winds up to our house. One afternoon, Leo visited the bar and had a coffee with the owner, and a fast friendship ensued. Franco knew all about Leo, and confessed that during the infamous 2012 conference in Roviano with Princess Kaorou and the gang, a new interest in his story resurfaced. Some of the audience got word that Franco lived nearby and paid him a visit, eager to hear about his experience..

In his 70s, he appeared a very mild mannered man. He spoke softly, and recounted his story to me in Italian. I grasped to understand the dialect, and nodded with a smile, my standard reaction when I don't understand something. Every village seemed to have a different dialect, even though we were only 30 minutes from Roviano, which put a strain on my understanding. I asked Leo later in the day to retell me everything It was a fascinating story about aliens and crystals and visions of forest people. I started constructing 2020 alien scenarios on my morning walk.

Leo left me alone for the first time in the house a couple of weeks after we moved in. He was attending his monthly Masonic meeting and I spent the evening watching movies. I went up to bed around 11 pm, not expecting Leo until at least 3 or 4 am. I tried to cuddle with Rambo, but he broke lose from my arms and perched on the edge of the bed, staring at the double doors of the closed balcony.

"What's wrong Rambo, come to bed," I urged.

I sat there for a second, perplexed, and that's when my right ear began to ring, and it was so loud I could barely stand it! I clasped my hand to my ear to try and muffle the sound as it vibrated through me. I noticed right away that the ringing in my ear had a rhythm, and it was changing pitch and vibrating. The room became hazy, as I clutched for my dog and held him close to me. We were both shaking and scared, but not sure of what. A light appeared from around the edges of the door. It was blue tinged and seemed to vibrate with the sound in my head.

Rambo was shaking like a leaf trying to break free from my grasp.

"What's going to happen now?"

Franco's story ran through my head. If I disappear for four days Leo is really going to freak out, I thought. The scene in the bedroom was only getting worse, I couldn't sit there another minute. My own voice sounded very far away, when I asked Rambo if he wanted to go outside. I was worried about him shaking so much. He jumped at the sound of my voice.

I'm sure the worst place to go if I was actually going to be abducted was the backyard, but that's what I did. As soon as I unlocked the back door and stepped out into the night air the ringing in my ear stopped. The UFO hovering over my house that I imagined was there, wasn't, only the stars scattered across the sky and the moonlit night greeted us. Running around in the grass broke the spell Rambo was under, as he seemed back to his old self again. I was relieved. I looked over at Alien mountain, lit up by the full moon, and peered over at the Holy Mary. *Something weird was going on around here!*When Leo came home that night from his Masonic meeting, he listened with interest, but I wasn't sure he believed me.

∞∞∞

A few weeks later, Leo awoke to a strange sound, but when he opened his eyes the house was quiet. I was sleeping and Rambo was sprawled out in the middle of the bed in his usual place. Leo said that he had listened for a moment or two before he heard the same vibrating sound I had described a few weeks ago. He told me it sounded mechanical and described the light under and around the balcony doors. He told me later that he waited for the sound to go away for a long time, before going back to sleep.

A few more experiences similiar to the ones I described above, happened in the winter when Tony came to visit for the first time. I continued to search the skies for something, *anything,* that resembled a space ship, but I never saw anything It was frustrating. The experiences only went as far as lights and sounds,and knowing what I know now, *I should be thankful for that!*

our new home.

My magical path.

Crystals and incense.

Even Rambo is grateful to be out of Roviano!

Chapter 37

London

W hen you think of London the imagination conjures up images of Buckingham Palace, double-decker buses, black cabs, Big Ben, and fish and chips. It has always been a city I dreamed of visiting, but the timing never seemed to be right, until now. One cold, January afternoon in 2018, we decided to book a weekend trip to London, and before we could change our minds our tickets were confirmed.

In late February, we headed to the airport, always excited for a new adventure. Leo was meeting a grandmaster in London, who offered to initiate me into Freemasonry. I never thought about becoming a Freemason, so the opportunity came as a complete surprise. Leo convinced me that if I joined we could attend the mixed lodge meetings in Sicily, so, it seemed that becoming a Freemason would be a chance for Leo and I to do more things together. I have to admit, I was curious to know the secrets and find out what the fuss was all about. Leo was initiated into the United Grand Lodge of England (UGLE) 10 years earlier, and he was very excited that I would be initiated in London, as well.

We arrived to cold sunny skies in Gatwick, which went against my preconceived vision of London fog. It had been pouring down rain for the last couple of days in Italy, and the temperature was dropping fast. The weather would prove to be even stranger as the days progressed. Europe was experiencing a cold front dubbed "The Beast from the East."

The smell of meat pies filled the air, as we raced through the old-fashioned train station. I felt like a heroine in a 40s film as I grabbed hold of Leo's hand and raced for the train. We squeezed in just before the doors closed, and I settled into my seat gazing dreamily out of the window at the English landscape that I was seeing for the first time.

Thirty minutes later, we were in Central London. I looked around with wide eyes, as I saw places that until now, I had only seen in movies. Leo was a great tour guide, announcing the different sites as we passed them. My heart beat excitedly as we whizzed by Hyde Park. Two men in suits on bicycles chatted with each other as they leisurely road their bikes side by side on the bike path that ran through the park. London was exactly how I imagined it to be, I expected to see Sherlock Holmes or James Bond at any moment! I was so thrilled I reached over and squeezed Leo's hand.

"Thank you for insisting we come, I love it already."

"London is great," Leo said with a smile.

The flat was cozy and charming, done up in true English fashion. The bed was comfy and we had everything we needed. I put down my bags and headed straight for the little kitchen. I scanned the cabinets for Italian coffee. I wanted to bring my own, but then thought better of it. With my luck it would have burst open and gotten all over Leo's suits. I had to take my chances that the flat, that was often frequented by Italians, would have good coffee available. My eyes scanned the pantry. *Bingo!* The same brand I used at home...and there was an oversized coffee machine on the counter. Having sorted out my coffee situation I took a quick tour of the apartment.

I was feeling pretty content as I unpacked my bag and settled in for what I hoped would be an exciting weekend. It had been so long since we traveled anywhere for fun. Day after day, week after week, month after month, for the past 4 years, we spent editing and translating Leo's books. I often found myself depressed because of it. I just wanted to relax and laugh and have fun.

We were starving, so we decided to head to the famous Lissons Fish and Chips that was conveniently located on the corner, for a late dinner. Princess Diana often brought her children there when they were little, and Leo said once he saw Beyonce pull up in a white limo and head for the take-away section of the restaurant. I ordered more food than I could eat, and more beer than I could drink, and in the end I only ate a quarter of my food. I was so tired, by the end of the meal I had to really push to keep my eyes open. I never sleep before I have to take a plane, and our flight had been early. I was looking forward to climbing into the comfy bed.

The next morning I made breakfast and we drank our coffee while watching English television. I left Leo laughing in the living room as I made my way to the bathroom to get ready for the day. As I lay in the bath, I tried to imagine what my initiation would be like. Passages from Leo's books crossed my mind, and they all involved blindfolds and knives. I had no idea what the initiation would entail, Leo didn't reveal any secrets to me and I didn't press him for details, because honestly, I was more concerned about what I was going to wear than what they would do to me. For this event, dark colors seemed like a good choice, and we both looked Masonic as we headed for the train station to take in some of London before our 4 o'clock lodge meeting.

Beautiful blue skies framed the typical English buildings, as I excitedly snapped pictures with my phone. It seemed like we had walked for miles, and I had seen half of London, before we decided to take a break for lunch. Leo arranged to meet one of his old DJ friends at his favorite Chinese restaurant from back in the day.

We were in Bayswater now, and Leo pointed to all of the rich homes, and said that this is where the celebrities hang out. Every shop I passed had something interesting in its window, a mass display of consumerism that I wasn't used to. The part of Italy that I lived in felt pretty basic in comparison. Of course, Milan and Rome are a different experience, but where we lived was pretty rustic. Most days we ate at the same restaurants that served the same traditional dishes, and we would buy just what we needed at the same shops. I used to be so materialistic, clothes and shoes and shopping for things that I really didn't need was one of my favorite past times. I am so glad I left that person behind!

Tired of all the shops, I turned to my phone and flipped through some of the pictures I had taken that morning, as we continued to walk toward the restaurant. At one point, Leo nudged me excitedly.

"Hey, I think that we just passed Keanu Reeves."

"Really? Where?" I asked, looking up excitedly.

I followed Leo's gaze, and a few feet away walking briskly in the opposite direction was a man that looked remarkably like Keanu Reeves! Tall with a long, dark trench coat flapping behind him, I contemplated running him down for an autograph, but thought better of it. Leo said they had made a silent exchange of knowing as they passed each other.

When we finally arrived at the Chinese restaurant, I googled the whereabouts of Keanu Reeves, and he *was* in London! Ah well... the photo of Leo meets Neo was lost. I drowned myself in Chinese beer and spring rolls and forgot all about it.

A windy day of sightseeing in London.

CHRISTY ZAGAMI

Elementary, my dear Watson!

The streets of London.

London at night.

Chapter 38

My initiation into Freemasonry

fter lunch, we headed back to the flat to quickly freshen up, and then we were off again. We were approaching Saturday night in London, and I could definitely feel the party vibe in the air. The evening was young, and crowds were lined up outside bars and pubs in anticipation of the night ahead.

I was feeling nervous, so I tried to distract myself by looking out of the window, we were near the Parliament area of London, and the scenery was different than what I had witnessed earlier in the day. We finally arrived at the designated meeting area, a Masonic pub located next to a very traditional looking English church where the lodge meeting would be held, and my initiation.

I wiped my sweaty palms on my skirt and exited the cab. For so many years, I watched Leo prepare for his lodge meetings where no women were allowed. I would joke and ask if I could come, and of course, the answer was always a resounding *"No!"* I painted a Masonic G and the Eye of Providence as a favor to Leo once for his lodge, but that was the extent of my participation in his, or any other Masonic lodge.

As we entered, the main part of the restaurant was alive with excitement, but we headed straight to the back, and through a door that led to a private room. The room was cozy and warm with a huge fireplace in the corner. Seated around a long table were 12 strangers, who eagerly looked up when we arrived. Forboding paintings of British aristocracy from past centuries seemed to scrutinize if we were worthy, as we greeted the others and found our place around the table. There were three women present, but they were engrossed in conversation, and only glanced our way briefly. Dressed in black from head to toe, I ended up nicknaming them, "*The three witches.*" I thought I was dressed somber, but I looked like Suzy Sunshine in comparison! The men at the table excitedly greeted Leo, A couple of them were from the Royal Arch, and some from the United Grand Lodge of England. One asked Leo to autograph a copy of his English book, Pope Francis, The Last Pope?

After sitting anxiously for an hour, the Grandmaster and his associate appeared in Masonic regalia, and told us the temple was ready, and to follow them. We exited a back door of the restaurant that led to a courtyard of the church. To outsiders we may have looked like a real Motley Cruel as we walked in procession towards the church, or maybe this was just business as usual on a Saturday night in the heart of London. Leo took my hand and squeezed it, trying to reassure me everything would be okay.

Me and another man in his late 20s were separated from the group and led to a room where we were told to wait. I frantically searched Leo's eyes, I didn't think we would be separated! He whispered, "*Don't worry,*" and kissed me goodbye. It was three hours before I would see him again.

The church in central London where my
Masonic initiation was held.

I made friends with my fellow initiate, as we spent three hours in a cold back room of the church, waiting expectantly, for what...we had no idea. He happened to be Russian and spoke German, and had the same love for Japan that I did. We laughed and joked and we almost forgot why we were there. A few times we put our ear to the closed door to see if we could hear anything coming from the inner recesses of the church. He didn't know what to expect, so I tried to fill him in by revealing everything I knew about initiations from Leo's books. When I mentioned the knife, he looked downright scared, but then I quickly laughed it off when I saw he really was nervous. Trying to appeal to his male side, I suggested that we could all wind up naked like in the movie "Eyes Wide Shut." That seemed to lighten his mood, as we patiently waited...*and waited.*

After what seemed like hours, and actually, it was, a very serious man arrived in a long robe and told us to follow him. My new Russian friend and I exchanged looks of trepidation. *This was it.* The night air whipped at our faces as we were led to the front of the church and an enormous wooden door. The Mason rapped on the door with a big brass knocker and someone I didn't recognize answered. We were then led into the entryway and separated. I wondered where Leo was, and if he was worried about me. We have never been apart for so long under such weird circumstances, but I had to trust that everything would be okay.

I can't disclose the details of my Masonic Inititation, but I can tell you some bits to give you an idea of what I went through. After meditating for some time on certain phrases and objects, we were led blindfolded and single file into the temple. I could hear my friend breathing, and I wondered if he could hear my heart beating. Loud booming voices recited history, and I felt thrust back to another time as extravagant theatrics were played out around me. At one point, hysterical cackles exploded, and I imagined it was the three witches really getting into their parts.

Ceremonial incense filled the air, as I tried to steady my nerves. All of a sudden, I was abruptly grabbed under my arm, a little too hard, I might add, as I was thrust this way and that. I knew after two seconds the man who grabbed me in the dark to lead me around was Leo. I felt better knowing he was there. He squeezed my breast at one point, and confessed to me later that he wanted to see how I would react if a stranger did that to me in the dark. I squinted my eyes at him, *"I knew it was you, dumb, dumb."*

Finally, the theatrics were over, and boy was I relieved! There were some moments that I truly felt thrust into a different time, and others where I was scared to death, even with Leo there. I felt proud of myself when I was given my apron and gloves and allowed to sit with the other Masons to attend the remainder of the Masonic meeting. Leo was the guest speaker, and I eagerly listened to his speech, watching the other members take in every word he said. I now shared a very special bond of brotherhood with these men and women, that I could never understand until now. I was a Freemason!

Chapter 39

Atlantis bookshop

We spent the remainder of our weekend in London sightseeing and eating. Leo insisted on quality, so it was the best Chinese, the best Indian, the best fish and chips, and so on. People complain that the food in England is terrible, but you have to know where to eat! On our last day, we met with a couple of organizers who wanted Leo to talk at a UFO conference that they were holding in May in a place called Watford, at an English Manor house. We agreed, and excitedly hugged each other when the meeting was over and the couple was out of view.

We would be returning to London in a couple of months for Leo's first conference in English. We spent years locked up in our dark apartment in Roviano working on the books, and now was our chance to interact with the public! We returned to Italy, but before we knew it we were packing our bags and heading back to London!

The conference was held on a Sunday, and we arrived on Friday. It was nice to know that we had time to relax before the event. We called Namastè kitchen the first night and had an Indian feast as we danced around in our matching Harry Potter pajamas that I bought just for the occasion.

We spent Saturday exploring the parts of London that I missed the first time, and after lunch we headed for an area called Seoul, where all the record shops are located, as well as Atlantis bookshop. Since our last trip to London, I had been nagging Leo that I wanted to visit the legendary bookshop that so many occultists from the past frequented, but Leo was hesitant to take me there.

"It's not your average bookshop, I have enemies there," Leo warned.

"But I just have to go, just to say I went. I can go in by myself, and you can hide around the corner," I excitedly replied as we jumped out of the cab that Leo directed to stop a block away from the notorious bookstore.

Some advice from Leo before entering the danger zone.

"Do you even pay attention to what you edit in my books?" Leo asked as we slowly headed toward the shop. *"These are my enemies, I wrote about them in Vol 2."*

I scanned my memory of the thousands and thousands of pages of text, but drew a blank.

"Don't worry, I won't dance around in there, I will be very discreet." I replied.

As we approached the brightly lit storefront with books displayed in the window and pretty flowers decorating the entry, I found nothing foreboding. We were sort of standing in the middle of the road, looking in, when Leo spotted three dark figures inside, and they were looking our way! He said each person by name to me, and I vaguely remembered what he had written in Vol 2.

Without another word, we approached the door and entered the small bookshop that was nothing like I had pictured from reading Dion Fortune's books. The three figures were now pretending to be busy talking to customers, and in a space that was so small there was barely any room to turn around, we headed toward the back of the store. The trio turned away, no greeting, no welcome, *they avoided our eyes*.

Leo pretended to browse the selection of esoteric books, while I headed further back into the deep labyrinth of the bookstore. As I approached a big painting of Dion Fortune surrounded by Baphomet statues, I felt invisible hands close around my throat, and and a force push me hard in my chest. I heard, *"GET OUT,"* so similar to the demon in Amityville Horror, the movie that caused me to spend what seemed like every night of my childhood with the bathroom light on and the bedroom door open.

I needed to leave. This place was toxic! I whizzed past Leo and told him we have to go, *now!* He followed me out and I didn't stop until I was down the block and around the corner, and that's when I threw up my lunch right there in the street! I told Leo what had happened, and I sensed his disappointment. I guess he wanted to make a stand in front of the OTO Satanists, but I just didn't feel up to confronting demons that day. I asked him if he felt okay, and he said that he prepared himself before he went in. He reminded me that he told me to do the same, but I admit I didn't listen. I even forgot the special protection crystal that I brought from home just for the occasion.

We spent the rest of the afternoon and evening visiting record shops, but I felt deeply depressed. Gone was the light happy mood I was in earlier in the day, replaced with a black funk that I couldn't shake. I decided to do my standard protection prayer, right there in the street, and I really didn't care who looked. I wanted to feel better, we had our conference the next day. After praying to all the angels and to the Holy Mary I began to feel a little lighter, but it took the rest of the day before I could shake away that horrible evil feeling.

Leo's attempt at being inconspicuous
Outside Atlantis bookshop, London.

The famous Atlantis bookshop in the heart of London, that has been frequented in the past by the world's most renowned occultists, to include Dion Fortune, Israel Regardie, and of course, the infamous Aleister Crowley.

Leo posing with a gargoyle in Chelsey.

The gates of Buckingham Palace, where are the bobbies?

Chapter 40

High Elms Manor

It seems fitting that I end my book with the UFO conference in London. The last nine years haven't been easy. Exposing the evil of the New World Order has left us vulnerable to attacks, on the material, as well as the spiritual realm. As you have read in the previous pages, it hasn't been easy! It's been a real battle, so arriving to High Elms Manor for Leo's first conference in the English language gave us a sense that we were beginning to reach people.

It was a beautiful Sunday afternoon when we arrived in the middle of the English countryside. The parking lot of the estate was packed with cars, there seemed to be a good turn out, which was exciting to see. You never really know who is going to show up for these conferences, and I remember events in Italy with less than 10 people, and that included me and Leo! This was definitely not the case at the UFO academy in Watford, you could feel the excitement in the air.

Loaded down with cases of books, we were greeted by the promoters of the conference, and made to feel comfortable and welcome. After setting up the books, we joined the others in the conference room. Leo took the stage to prepare, and I scanned the room, trying to figure out where to put myself. I spotted an attractive young woman with good energy in the middle row, sitting by herself, so I decided to sit next to her.

We were swept into a world of mystery and intrigue as Leo explained the connection between the UFO phenomenon and the extradimensional realm. Leo has a way of really captivating an audience, and although I knew everything he was talking about, I was sorry when his talk was over. I wanted to know more, and so did everyone else, but unfortunately our time had come to an end, and the next speaker was taking the stage. I sold almost all of the books we brought, and Leo was able to engage with his fans, people that had come from all over England to hear him speak. For me, it was a very fulfilling experience to finally talk to people about spirituality and psychic protection. In the past, I could only manage a smile at the conferences in Italy, as my Italian skills were never up to par. It was a great feeling to finally be able to express myself, and I hope that together with Leo, we can reach many more people in the future.

There is a quote: *In vain you have acquired knowledge, if you have not imparted it on others...*and we intend to do just that!

photo credit: Miriam Benko.

It was great to see Infowarriors at the event!

Conclusion

The adventures in this book have taught me to fight for what I believe in, even though at times I wanted to run and hide. I had to find the courage inside myself, and I wouldn't take back one moment of what I have experienced so far, because even in the most difficult of times, there was always a lesson to be learned. There is a quote, *do small things with great love,* and that is how I try to live my life every day.

In a little alcove outside of my window stands a statue of the Virgin Mary. Her graceful beauty is a gentle reminder, that as long as I believe, I can achieve anything I want in life, and so can you! If there is someone out there that is struggling, but can find inspiration in my words, then this book has served its purpose. Remember, that every day counts so try to live every moment to its fullest. It's never too late to make a new start, no matter how desperate your situation. You can be anyone you want to be as long as you believe in yourself. *That is where true magic lies.*

It is better to conquer yourself than to win a thousand battles. Then the victory is yours. It cannot be taken from you, not by angels or by demons, heaven or hell- Buddha

Until we meet again,
Christy Zagami 5-16-18

Made in United States
Orlando, FL
05 March 2024